DEVELOPING

W9-BDH-324

3
Simple Truths
and

6
Essential Traits
of

Powerful Writing

PRESTWICK HOUSE, INC.
"Everything for the English Classroom!"

Simple Truths
and

Essential Traits
of

Powerful Writing

SENIOR EDITOR: Douglas E. Grudzina

EDITOR: Mary C. Beardsley

BOOK DESIGN: Larry Knox

PRODUCTION: Jerry Clark

PRESTWICK HOUSE, INC.

P.O. Box 658 • Clayton, Delaware 19938
TEL: 1.800.932.4593
FAX: 1.888.718.9333
WEB: www.prestwickhouse.com

ISBN 978-1-58049-321-5

Table of Contents

Book

Continued on next page

Applying *the* Third Truth

Powerful writing is painless to read.

A PPENDIX

DEVELOPING

Simple Truths
and

Essential Traits
of

Powerful Writing

PRESTWICK HOUSE, INC.

"Everything for the English Classroom!"

Essential Traits

OVER THE PAST SEVERAL YEARS, two trends in writing instruction have grown in popularity: primary trait instruction and trait-based scoring. Both of these trends carry great benefits for the students, but their effectiveness is limited by how they are understood and implemented in today's classrooms. The Prestwick House *Simple Truths* series hopes to overcome a few of these limitations.

Primary Trait Instruction comes packaged under a number of names, and is probably the most popular method of teaching writing. It is based on the premise that there are six (some editors opt for five traits while others promote seven traits; we feel six cover writing instruction best) essential characteristics or "traits" to a piece of writing and that each of these traits can be taught separately. These traits can then be combined, at some point, to produce a good essay.

Throughout the *Simple Truths* series, we will focus on the traits of **Development and Elaboration, Organization, Sentence Structure and Variety, Conventions of Written English, Word Choice,** and **Voice**. Each of these is explained in its own chapter.

Underlying the Six Essential Traits, however, are three simple principles, or truths, that *explain the need* for each of the traits in powerful writing.

A Review of the Three Truths:

As we discussed in the first book of the *Three Simple Truths* series, any piece of writing can be analyzed in terms of six essential traits: Development and Elaboration, Organization, Sentence Structure and Variety, Conventions of Written English, Word Choice, and Voice. None of these traits, however, exists for its own purpose, but each is important in how it helps the writing to follow three simple truths of powerful writing.

1st Truth	Powerful writing really says something.

ESSENTIAL TRAIT:

❶ Development and Elaboration

Your writing needs a point and must contain important information you want to share with someone else.

2nd Truth	Powerful writing is understandable to others.

ESSENTIAL TRAITS:

❷ Organization

❸ Sentence Structure and Variety

❹ Conventions of Written English

You are writing to communicate your main idea with another person or other people. You will not be with the reader to explain what you mean, so what you write must be clear and understandable to your reader.

3rd Truth	Powerful writing is painless to read.

ESSENTIAL TRAITS:

❺ Word Choice

❻ Voice

You certainly do *not* want your essay to be a painful experience for your reader. You do *not* want your essay to be the 200th bad essay the potential employer, test scorer, or college admissions official has read that day. You want your essay to be painless—preferably even enjoyable—to read.

BOOK TWO: DEVELOPING

Applying
the
First Truth

Powerful writing really says something.

3
Simple Truths
and
6
Essential Traits
of

Powerful Writing

DEVELOPMENT AND ELABORATION

Trait
One

TRAIT ONE:
DEVELOPMENT AND ELABORATION

Every successful piece of nonfiction should leave the reader with one provocative thought that he or she didn't have before. Not two thoughts, or five—just one.

Decide what corner of your subject you're going to bite off, and be content to cover it well and stop.

—William Zinsser, *On Writing Well*

Identifying and Narrowing Your Topic

Since elementary school, your teachers probably have admonished you to "narrow down your topic." You might have understood this to mean that you could not write about the entire elephant, but had to focus on, say, the elephant's trunk.

What your teachers have been asking you, however, is if you want to write about elephants, what *one point* about elephants do you want to make? The key to offering your reader a "full and complete discussion" necessary for a score of 8 on the Development and Elaboration rubric, is to "bite off no more than you can chew and digest" in the amount of time and space you are allowed.

For example, you might want to establish for your reader:

- elephants make excellent house pets;
- elephants should not be confined in zoos and circuses;
- endangered elephant species need to be protected by international law.

After you identify your one point, you then need to decide how much you want to cover. (This might actually mean how much you can cover in the time and space you are allowed.)

If you find countless reasons why elephants make excellent house pets, you may find you need to focus your essay on:

- how easy elephants are to care for;
- how elephants are good company for the elderly and the shut-in;
- how protective elephants can be of children.

After you've identified the one point you will establish and the extent to which you will establish it, then you can begin to look for the facts and examples you will use to establish your point.

Make Yours Better!

Note that the main problem with the following essay is it lacks Development and Elaboration.

■ The introduction gives us three ideas that the essay could be about, but does not clearly identify the main idea.

■ The second paragraph gives us a series of facts which do not develop the ideas in the introduction.

■ The third paragraph wanders away from the topic of the rishis, returning only at the end.

The sacred Hindu literature known as the Vedas are divided into four main parts: Rig, Sama, Yajur, and Atharva. They are considered revealed literature because they are based on what was heard by the rishis, or prophets. "Revealed literature" is a term for those writings which are considered direct communication from a divine source to a human recorder.

A rishi can be any person who sings a sacred song or is inspired to write poetry. Some rishis were supposed to have heard the divine truth of the Vedas during religious ceremonies. The term is used specifically for the authors of the Rigveda. Famous rishis include Paili, Vaishampayana, and Jaimini. One of the most important rishis, Vyasa, whose name means "Splitter," was supposed to have shown people how to split up the Vedas so that they could be understood.

People who believe in the Vedas religiously believe that they have existed since the beginning of creation, even though they were heard by the rishis at some point in time. The Sanskrit term for revealed literature is sruti. This term refers to all of the revealed literature in Hinduism, from the beginning to the present. It literally means "what is heard." In Hinduism, the cosmic truth of the universe is heard by the rishis.

In the religions of the world, sacred truths are believed to have been revealed through different methods. The words of Jesus, whom Christians believe to be the son of God, were written down by disciples, or followers. Mormon religion teaches that revealed truth can be found by anyone who seeks it, not just a special priest. Only Hinduism features the special rishis, who are both priests and prophets.

▨ **The conclusion introduces new information and does not sum up the essay's main point.**

Essay Critique

This passage lacks a clear thesis statement, so it is difficult to determine what the author's main idea is. Although there is an abundance of interesting information here, the author should make sure that all the supporting sentences contribute to the main idea.

This essay receives a score of **4** on the:

Development and Elaboration Rubric

8 = The main idea of the essay is clear. There is almost enough information for a full and complete discussion, but the reader is left with a few unanswered questions. Minor irrelevancies, redundancies, and superfluencies weaken the overall impact of the essay.

7 = ADVANCING
The main idea of the essay is clear. Every supporting point is supported and details are elaborated upon, but minor irrelevancies, redundancies, and superfluencies weaken the overall impact of the essay.

6 = The main idea of the essay is clear, most supporting points are elaborated upon, but some of the information presented is notably irrelevant, redundant, and superfluous.

5 = The main idea of the essay is clear, but the overall discussion is weakened by inconsistent development and elaboration. Some Supporting points tend to be underdeveloped (too few details, examples, anecdotes, supporting facts, etc.). Some minor irrelevancies likewise weaken the essay.

4 = DEVELOPING
The main idea of the essay is suggested. There are supporting details with some elaboration, but supporting points are underdeveloped. Some of the points or development my be tangential or irrelevant to the topic, purpose, and audience.

Exercise 1: Identifying a Main Idea and Drafting a Thesis

Think about a book you have read or a movie you have seen, preferably one that is readily available to you so that you can reread or re-watch portions as necessary.

1. *In one sentence,* state the theme or meaning of the book or movie.

   Example:
   The experiences of Alex the Lion in DreamWorks animated film Madagascar *illustrate the theme that civilization is merely a thin veneer, and one is never too far from revealing one's brutal nature.*

2. *In one sentence,* evaluate the main character.

   Example:
   Alex the Lion, one of the main characters in the DreamWorks animated film Madagascar, *is a truly decent fellow painfully caught between his desire to be "good" and the increasingly irresistible call of his inner nature.*

3. *In one sentence,* describe *how* the book or movie is put together (written, filmed, formatted) better than or differently from other books you have read or movies you have seen.

   Example:
   The 2005 DreamWorks animated film Madagascar *takes the science of computer animation to a new level that other studios will find hard to match.*

Exercise 2: Brainstorming Illustrative Details and Evidence

After drafting your thesis, it is helpful to brainstorm and list the facts, details, examples, etc., that you suspect you will need in order to discuss your main idea fully. Perhaps you will need to look again at the book or movie you are writing about in order to find enough facts and details for the piece you are writing.

Jot down the facts, details, and other ideas you might use to develop each of the theses you drafted above.

For example:

Thesis: *The experiences of Alex the Lion in DreamWorks animated film Madagascar illustrate the theme that civilization is merely a thin veneer, and one is never too far from revealing one's brutal nature.*

- *Alex is a meat eater (even in New York)*

- *Does not have to hunt in New York*

- *Well-fed, no threat to friends*

- *Well-fed, does not consider friends to be prey*

- *On island, experiences hunger*

- *Is appalled at viewing his friends (Melman) as food*

- *Cannot control his carnivorous urges*

- *Voluntarily separates self from his friends*

Thesis: Thesis: Thesis:

-
-
-
-
-
-
-

Taking and Organizing Notes

Reread the "Make Yours Better" essay on page 12. Even though it is underdeveloped and the main point is somewhat unclear, there is some good information there. Some of that information might have come from knowledge the writer had already gained from prior learning. Most of it was probably gained by research the writer performed for the purpose of writing the essay. None of it is personal observation, reflection, or opinion. The point is, a good deal of your writing is going to be based on research.

Now, research is really not a big deal. When you access a website to check movie listings in your area, you are doing research. When you look up a number in the phone book, you are doing research. When you call a store to find out what time they close, or whether or not they carry a particular item, you are doing research. When you ask your teacher or a parent how to spell a word you don't feel like looking up, you are doing research.

So, research is simply the gathering of information from various sources for your purpose.

The key to good research lies in three things: finding and using good sources, finding and using enough sources, and taking good notes. The first two will be discussed in the next book, but we will begin thinking about taking and organizing notes from research here.

You've already been through two stages of writing development. When you first started learning to write, your information source was you. Your essays were largely personal reflections, personal accounts of field trips you'd taken, experiences you'd had, etc.

Then, you began to write reports in which you consulted one or more "outside" sources and simply repeated the information you got.

The next step is to combine information from outside sources with information you already know and to create new information in the process.

For the next couple of exercises, you'll need several 3" X 5" index cards and three different colors of writing utensil (for example, a pencil, a blue pen, and a red pen). Then, consider that you will take three different types of notes: information directly from the source; information you already know; and your own observations, insights, or original ideas inspired by your source. You'll use three different colors to write your notes, one for each of the three types of sources. All notes based on information you already know will be written in one color, all those from outside sources will be another, and the notes based on your own original ideas will be a third color. This will allow you to *see* that your essay or paper is an appropriate blend of outside information and your own insight.

A **NOTE ABOUT NOTE CARDS:** With the introduction of higher technology into the classroom, some "old fashioned" research and writing methods have fallen into disfavor, note cards among them. However, modern wonders like the Internet and word processing—with the ability simply to copy information from a website and paste it into your own paper—have resulted in rampant charges of plagiarism. Some of these charges are warranted; others are undeserved, in the event that the accused student did not know he or she was committing a crime. One of the best ways to avoid actually committing plagiarism and to defend yourself against unjust charges of plagiarism—which can result in your being expelled from your college or graduate school—is to be able to present a file of notes—in your own handwriting—that correspond to your outline and to your paper.

Look again at the list of information provided as the example for Exercise 2. Notice that, while there are a few sentences, most of the notes are simply fragments that contain the pertinent information. Notice, too, that, in the example, there are only facts, no evaluation, judgment, opinion, or personal insight. If these were notes, they would all be in whatever color you chose to indicate information taken directly from an outside source—in this case, the source is the movie.

Each bulleted fact would be its own note, on its own index card.

Exercise 3: Reading and Taking Notes

The following passage is about Christopher Columbus's four journeys to the North American continent—not terribly exciting, but something about which you already know some things. Have your 3" X 5" cards ready. Before you read the passage, take notes on what you already know—or think you know—about Columbus and his journeys. Remember to write these notes in the color you've selected for information you already know.

Also take notes on any questions you have or any opinions or insights you believe you have that you might want to share in a paper on Christopher Columbus. Write these notes in whatever color you have chosen for your own opinions and insights.

After you have brainstormed and taken notes, read the passage, taking notes in the color you have chosen for information taken directly from a source. If, while you read, you generate some new ideas, form some new opinions, or develop some insights, note them on index cards in the appropriate color.

Ready? Now, take notes as you read the following selection:

All told, Christopher Columbus—who was born in Italy, and whose name was really Cristoforo Colombo—made four voyages to what Europeans called "The New World" between 1492 and 1504. Once celebrated as the "Discoverer" of America and the hero of western history, and later derided as a genocidal mass murderer and the scourge of the indigenous peoples of the Americas, Columbus was actually somewhere in between, an intelligent adventurer and shrewd negotiator with perhaps something of a mean streak.

Columbus's first voyage—his famous voyage of "discovery"—began at the port of Palos in southern Spain, on August 3, 1492. Everyone knows the story of Columbus seeking funding from Queen Isabella and King Ferdinand of Spain, with which he secured and outfitted his three ships: the well-known *Niña*, *Pinta*, and *Santa Maria*.

The first port of call for this expedition was at the Canary Islands, which were, at the time, the westernmost Spanish possessions. Calm winds and the need to repair his vessels caused a four-week delay there. He was finally able to resume his voyage on September 6, 1492, although calm winds still kept him in sight of the westernmost Canary Island for two more days.

Columbus arrived at what is now the Bahama Islands on October 12, the day now celebrated as Columbus Day. He proceeded to Cuba on October 28. While sailing north of Cuba on November 22, the captain of the *Pinta* left the other two ships, without permission, to search for an island called "Babeque," where he believed he would find much gold. Columbus continued eastward with the *Santa Maria* and *Niña*, arriving at Hispaniola on December 5.

The flagship *Santa Maria* hit a reef on Christmas Eve and sank the next day. Columbus used the remains of the ship to build a fort on shore, which he named *La Navidad* (for Christmas). With the earlier loss of the renegade *Pinta*, the tiny *Niña* was now Columbus's only ship. She was too small to hold all of the remaining crew, so Columbus was forced to leave about 40 men at La Navidad to wait for his return from Spain. He left La Navidad to return to Spain on January 2, 1493.

He accidentally reconnected with Pinzón and the *Pinta*, but they were again separated by a storm, each believing the other to have perished. Columbus eventually made it back to his home port of Palos on March 15, 1493. Pinzón and the Pinta arrived only a few hours after the *Niña*. Pinzón had expected to be proclaimed a hero, but the honor had already been bestowed on Columbus. Pinzón died a few days later.

After the success of his first voyage, Columbus easily convinced Ferdinand and Isabela to allow a second voyage. Whereas the first voyage had been for the purpose of exploration, this second was to begin a massive colonization effort. The rulers of Spain paid for seventeen ships and over a thousand men. This second voyage brought European horses, sheep, and cattle to the New World for the first time.

The fleet left the Canary Islands on October 13, 1493, intending to land at Hispaniola, where Columbus had left 40 men the previous January. They sighted land in the West Indies on Sunday, November 3—a mere twenty-one days from their launch from Spain.

During the next two weeks, the fleet sailed north "discovering" the Leeward Islands, the Virgin Islands, and Puerto Rico before arriving at Hispaniola on November 22.

When he returned to La Navidad on November 28, Columbus found that the fort had been burned, and the men he had left there were dead. According to the local chief, the men at Navidad argued among themselves over women and gold. Some of the men abandoned the fort, and some of the others raided an inland tribe, kidnapping their women. The men of that tribe retaliated by destroying the fort and killing the Spaniards.

Leaving the site of his first attempt at settlement, Columbus sailed eastward along the coast of Hispaniola, looking for a place to found his colony. On December 8, he anchored and founded a new town he named *La Isabela*, after the Spanish queen. He spent the next several months establishing the colony and exploring the interior of Hispaniola.

Columbus still insisted that he had sailed to the Far East, and that the mainland of China was nearby. Therefore, on April 24, 1494, he left La Isabela with three ships. He reached what is now Cuba on April 30. He then learned of an island to the south that was supposedly rich with gold. Columbus left Cuba on May 3rd and anchored at Jamaica two days later. The natives, however, were mostly hostile and, since

Columbus's goal was the mainland of China, he left Jamaica on May 13, returning to Cuba the next day.

Due to the nature of the southern coast, however, exploration of Cuba proved to be too difficult and treacherous. On June 13, Columbus abandoned the quest. He did not, however, want to admit that his search for the mainland had been a failure, so he had every man in his crew sign a document and swear that Cuba was so large, it had to be the mainland.

Navigating the treacherous coast of Cuba made their return to Hispaniola difficult and slow, so they again sailed to Jamaica to verify that it was indeed an island. On August 20, 1494, they finally returned to Hispaniola and explored the southern coast. By the end of September, Columbus was seriously ill, so his crew abandoned their exploration and returned to La Isabela. On March 10, 1496, Columbus left La Isabela to return to Spain. He sighted the coast of Portugal on June 8.

Columbus's third voyage began on May 30, 1498. This time, he'd been equipped with six ships. After stopping again at the Canary Islands, the fleet split into two squadrons. Three of the ships sailed directly for Hispaniola with supplies for the colonists. The other three, commanded by Columbus himself, explored the waters in an attempt to find any additional land south of the islands they had already discovered.

The fleet was delayed in the Doldrums, an area at the equator, off the coast of Africa, famous for its lack of winds. By the time winds returned eight days later, the fleet's fresh water was running out, so they set sail directly to Dominica, the island Columbus had "discovered" on his second voyage. That same day, the crew sighted an island that had three hills. Columbus—a devoutly religious man—named the island "Trinidad" after the Holy Trinity.

While the fleet was taking on drinking water in Trinidad, they sighted the coast of South America, becoming the first Europeans to see that continent. For the next week, Columbus explored the Gulf of Paria that lies between South America and Trinidad. Columbus grew ill, and the fleet finally sailed to Hispaniola.

At the new city of Santo Domingo, Columbus learned that unhappy colonists had staged a revolt against his rule. The colonists' grievances all sprang from the fact that Columbus considered all of his "discovered" territory to be his own personal domain, and he tried to control every aspect of the colony's economy—even when he was not present to appreciate fully their needs and concerns.

Columbus was unable to put down the revolt, and was forced to agree to peace. As the rumors of limitless gold began to appear terribly exaggerated, everyone—colonists and Ferdinand and Isabella of Spain—grew increasingly unhappy. The rulers appointed Francisco de Bobadilla as "Royal Commissioner," whose powers were even greater than Columbus's. As soon as he arrived in Santo Domingo, he had Columbus arrested and shipped back to Spain.

Christopher Columbus's fourth and final voyage was perhaps his most interesting and exciting. Still convinced that he had sailed around the globe and arrived at Asia, he wanted to find the strait connecting the Pacific and Indian Oceans that Marco Polo described in his travels. The strait Columbus was seeking was the Strait of Malacca, which is near Singapore in the Pacific Ocean!

A fleet of four old ships and 140 crew members set sail on May 11, 1502. On this voyage, the crew included Columbus's brother Bartholomew, as well as Columbus's younger son Fernando, who was thirteen years old. Columbus himself was fifty-one years old and in poor health. He insisted, however, on making this one last voyage.

The fleet arrived at Santo Domingo on June 29, 1502 and requested permission to enter the harbor for protection from an approaching storm. Columbus also warned that the treasure fleet preparing to leave should stay put until the storm had passed. Because dissatisfaction over Columbus's governance of his colony was still strong on Hispaniola, his request for shelter was rudely denied. Also, despite the experienced sailor and explorer's warnings, the thirty ships laden with treasure sailed on their way to Spain. Columbus found shelter for his ships nearby.

A hurricane hit, and the treasure fleet was caught at sea. Twenty ships sank. Nine others barely managed to return to Santo Domingo. Only one of the thirty made it safely to Spain. Columbus's four ships all survived the storm.

At the end of July, Columbus arrived at the coast of Honduras and spent the next two months working his way down the coast, his progress impeded by still more storms and strong headwinds. When they arrived at what is now Panama, the natives told them that there was another ocean just a few days' march to the south. This convinced Columbus that he was indeed near Marco Polo's strait, and further convinced him that he had sailed to the Indies.

The fleet continued exploring and searching for the rich gold deposits they had heard about until more storms and winds forced Columbus to settle in western Panama where he built a garrison fort near the mouth of the Rio Belen. When he prepared to leave for Spain, he sailed three of his ships out of the river, leaving the fourth with the garrison. The next day, at low tide, the river was so low that the fourth boat was trapped by a sandbar. Seizing the opportunity, a large force of natives attacked the garrison.

The Spanish managed to hold off the attack, but lost a number of men and realized that the garrison was by no means secure. Columbus abandoned the ship in the river and rescued the remaining members of the garrison. The three ships—badly leaking from shipworm—sailed for home on April 16.

One of the remaining ships had to be abandoned almost immediately because it was no longer seaworthy, and the remaining two tried desperately to make it to Hispaniola. Off the coast of Cuba, however, they were hit by yet another storm. The last of the ship's boats was lost, and one of the two remaining vessels was so badly damaged that she had to be towed by the flagship. Both ships were leaking very badly. Finally, no longer able to keep them afloat, Columbus beached the sinking ships in St.

Anne's Bay, Jamaica, on June 25, 1503. With no Spanish colony on Jamaica, they were marooned.

One of Columbus's captains bought a canoe from a local chief and sailed it to Hispaniola, where he was immediately detained by governor for seven months. The governor also denied the request of a small ship to rescue the rest of the men stranded in Jamaica.

Meanwhile, half of those left on Jamaica mutinied against Columbus. On Santo Domingo, the detained captain was finally granted permission to enter the city and managed to charter a small ship, which arrived at Jamaica on June 29, 1504. Columbus returned home to Spain on November 7, 1504, his last voyage complete. He died on May 20, 1506.

Review all of the notes you have taken, and write a thesis statement for a paper about Christopher Columbus. Save the passage, your notes, and your thesis statement for a later exercise.

Thesis:

Developing Ideas by Showing Rather Than Telling

Below is a famous drawing titled "My Wife and My Mother-in-Law," originally published in 1915 by cartoonist W.E. Hill. You'll probably recognize it as one of those "trick" drawings that show two different objects, depending on how the viewer sees it. In this case, Mr. Hill's "wife" is a young woman wearing a fur stole, elegant veil, and ostrich feather. There is a choker-necklace around her neck, and she is turned mostly away from the viewer. The "mother-in-law" is much older. She is also wearing a fur and a plume, but the viewer sees her full profile, and she has a rather large nose and prominent chin.

Most people, when they look at this picture, immediately see either the wife or the mother-in-law. When told that there is another woman also in the picture, most people are able to see it by shifting their focus. There are, however, those people who cannot see the "other woman" without someone actually pointing out the individual features: here is the nose, here is her ear, this is her necklace, etc.

How you present this image to someone else illustrates the difference between "telling" and "showing."

"Telling" is merely saying what features are there. "Showing" is actually pointing the features out.

Look at the following paragraph that *tells* the reader about the cartoon:

> The famous cartoon "My Wife and My Mother-in-Law," published in 1915 by cartoonist W.E. Hill, is a double-image illusion that simultaneously illustrates both a beautiful young woman and an elderly crone. The beautiful young woman, presumably the "wife," is wearing a fur stole, an elegant veil, and an ostrich feather. There is a choker-style necklace around her neck, and she is turned mostly away from the viewer. The "mother-in-law" is much older. She is also wearing a fur and a plume, but the viewer sees her full profile. She has a rather large nose and prominent chin.

There is nothing wrong with this paragraph. In fact, it is not a bad introduction to a longer essay about the cartoon. Its main flaw, however, is that—if its purpose is to give the reader a clear and complete understanding of the image—it fails. The paragraph *tells* the reader what is in the image, but does not *show* the reader what is there.

Now look at the following paragraph that does a much better job of *showing* the reader how the illusion works.

> The famous cartoon "My Wife and My Mother-in-Law," published in 1915 by cartoonist W.E. Hill, is a double-image illusion that simultaneously illustrates both a beautiful young woman and an elderly crone. In the image, both women are wearing furs, depicted by the dark areas that fill nearly the entire bottom half of the image. The old woman—presumably the "mother-in-law"—is wearing the fur much higher around her neck, so that the white space dividing the "fur" is the old woman's prominent chin and the young woman's upper chest and neck. The old woman's toothless mouth is the younger woman's choker-style necklace. The old woman is sitting full-profile to the viewer, while the young woman is turned away. Thus, what is the "mother-in-law's" nose is the "wife's" neck, jawline, and cheek, and the old woman's left eye is the young woman's left ear. Both women have dark, curly hair, but the wife's hair is dressed with a veil flowing down the back of her head, while the mother-in-law has covered most of her hair in a kerchief. Most viewers instantly see one view or the other. But with a little shift in focus, and maybe a little prompting, they can see both the wife and the mother-in-law and marvel at cartoonist W.E. Hill's cleverness.

This second paragraph is longer, due to a detailed description, *showing* the reader the features of each aspect of the image.

Exercise 4: Developing a Main Idea

*Each of the following items states a main idea and begins to develop it. The development, however, is vague and lacks details. In other words, it **tells** rather than **shows**. For each example, list some specific facts, details, or examples you could use to **show** your reader the validity of the main idea. (For the purposes of this exercise, it is all right if you need to make up "facts.")*

For example:
Viewing a movie based on a novel cannot be considered a valid replacement for reading the novel. Filmmakers often take liberties with the original story, deleting characters or plot events, changing settings, even changing the focus and theme of the novel.

Details/Examples:
Slaughterhouse-Five: in movie, character of Kilgore Trout is deleted, and Valencia's car accident-death scene is greatly expanded to add comedy. Events in novel are completely as Billy experienced them; movie shows German boy running to burning ruins of apartment house in search of his dead girl-friend, an event Billy had no knowledge of. The Great Gatsby: everything in novel is filtered through Nick's viewpoint. The Robert Markowitz television adaptation (2000), however, includes many flashbacks of Daisy and Gatsby's earlier relationship: their meeting, parting, etc.

1. Exercising daily is a healthy habit to establish. People who exercise are generally happier and healthier, and lead much more productive lives than couch potatoes.

Details/Examples:

2. The United States has become largely a nation of complainers. The frivolous lawsuits that daily choke our justice system are proof of this.

Details/Examples:

3. Elderly people should own pets. There are many emotional, psychological, and physical health benefits to owning and caring for an animal.

Details/Examples:

4. A great deal of evidence suggests that, while reality T.V. shows may appear to be unscripted and spontaneous, in truth, they are really carefully planned and staged dramas. Only the most emotional episodes are broadcast, and the cameo-interview segments are carefully edited to highlight conflict.

Details/Examples:

5. There are times when teenagers and adults simply do not understand each other. Too often, the two generations do not listen to each other or consider the validity of the other's viewpoint.

Details/Examples:

Exercise 5: Developing Ideas from Other Content Areas

Consider what you are currently studying in your other academic classes and do the following:

Note an idea or concept you've studied this week with which you agree.

Note an idea or concept you've studied this week with which you disagree.

Note an idea or concept you've studied this week which you find especially interesting.

Note an idea or concept you've studied this week that you do not fully understand.

For the idea or concept with which you agree, answer the following questions:

How much do you know about this subject?

What is the basis of your agreement?

What evidence can you offer to support your opinion?

List the source(s) for this evidence:

What evidence exists to support the opposite opinion?

List the source(s) for this evidence:

How can you refute this evidence?

For the idea or concept with which you disagree, answer the following questions:

How much do you know about this subject?

What is the basis of your disagreement?

What evidence can you offer to support your opinion?

List the source(s) for this evidence:

What evidence exists to support the opposite opinion?

List the source(s) for this evidence:

How can you refute this evidence?

For the idea or concept you find particularly interesting, answer the following questions:

Is this new knowledge or something you knew before?

What do you find interesting about it?

What background information would you have to give to a reader in order to explain this?

Writing Opportunity: *The Writing Assessment Essay: Responding to a Quotation*

Because tens of thousands of students take standardized tests, most of the writing questions on tests like the SAT and your state's writing assessment, will be very general, not relying on any specific knowledge. Therefore, many of these writing exams simply ask you to respond to a quotation from a work of literature or a great historical figure.

Depending on the assessment, you might have as little as twenty minutes to write your essay, or as long as an hour or two. The key to success on this type of assessment, then, is getting and developing an idea as fully as you can as quickly as you can. All of the traits of powerful essays are important in a writing assessment, but—while your scorer may be instructed to forgive the occasional spelling or grammatical error—you will be heavily penalized if you have nothing to say. Therefore, Development and Elaboration is probably the most important trait in this setting.

Below, is a writing prompt similar to ones you are likely to encounter on the SAT or state writing assessment.

Remember to apply the techniques you learned in this chapter to develop a main idea and then offer as many specific details in support of that main idea as you can.

Prompt: *Read the following quotation, and then write an essay in which you agree or disagree with Twain's observation about happiness.*

> *Happiness ain't a thing in itself—it's only a contrast with something that ain't pleasant.... And so, as soon as the novelty is over and the force of the contrast dulled, it ain't happiness any longer, and you have to get something fresh.*
>
> *—Mark Twain*

Step 1: *Develop your thesis*

What is Twain saying about happiness? First, rephrase the quotation in your own words to be sure you understand what he has said. Then, decide whether your initial reaction is to agree or disagree.

Step 2: *Brainstorm your supporting ideas and details*

Whether you agree or disagree with Twain's statement, ask yourself "why?" Consider events you've experienced, witnessed, read, or heard about that support your position.

Time Clue: Because of the nature of most writing assessments, you won't want to spend more than a few minutes on these early steps. For a 30-minute essay, you'll want to spend no more than a minute to decide whether you agree or disagree, and another five minutes to brainstorm your examples and details.

Hint: If examples and details do not come to you immediately, change your stance (e.g., from agreeing with the quotation to disagreeing with the quotation) and then brainstorm.

Step 3: *Draft your introductory paragraph*

Use the five-paragraph essay format as a default structure. Write your thesis (statement of agreement or disagreement) and three or four sentences indicating the examples you will be discussing.

Time Clue: For a 30-minute essay, allow yourself approximately five minutes for this first paragraph.

Step 4: *Draft your supporting paragraphs*
Make them as good as you can. You have already brainstormed these details, so this is framing them into sentences and paragraphs. Write one paragraph for each of the supporting details in your introduction.

Chances are, this will be your *only* draft—so make it good.

Time Clue: Give yourself 10 – 15 minutes for this step. If you did a good enough job in Steps 2 and 3, writing these paragraphs will be a breeze.

Step 5: *Draft your concluding paragraph*
Depending on time, this needs to be nothing more than a summation of your thesis and the details you used to establish it. Introduce it with a quick transition like "thus" or "therefore."

Time Clue: Depending on the assessment, time will probably be called during this step.

DO NOT PANIC IF TIME IS CALLED, AND YOU HAVE NOT FINISHED YOUR ESSAY.

Scorers of many large-scale essay assessments are told to "reward what's there" rather than penalize for what is not there. This means that, if you have established that you know how to frame a thesis statement and write an introduction, and the paragraphs you managed to write give evidence that you know how to elaborate on that introduction, you will probably receive a satisfactory score.

Step 6: *Reread and revise your essay*
If time allows, double-check your essay to clean up any spelling or minor grammatical errors you may find. Chances are you won't have time for a full second draft, but do take the time to make this draft as clean as possible.

Applying
the
SECOND Truth

Powerful writing is understandable to others.

3
Simple Truths
and

6
Essential Traits
of

Powerful Writing

Organization

Trait
Two

TRAIT TWO:
ORGANIZATION

All writing is organized. Again, at the NOVICE and DEVELOPING levels, we strongly recommend that you master the basic five-paragraph essay format. As you ascend the scale and approach the PROFICIENT and ACCOMPLISHED levels, you will discover more sophisticated ways to organize your essays and longer papers.

Review of the Five-Paragraph Essay

The five-paragraph essay is a basic structure in which the first paragraph is the introduction that includes your main idea or thesis and the three main sub-points you are going to develop.

The following three paragraphs each introduce one of the three sub-points and develop it with facts, examples, etc.

The fifth paragraph is the conclusion that wraps up the discussion, gives an overview of the development, and establishes the validity of the thesis.

A Note of Caution: One of the problems the five-paragraph essay presents to developing writers is that it may lead them to the conclusion that they can develop only three sub-points of their thesis.

You might have only two strong points of development, or you might actually have four or five (or more) strong points of development. What the five-paragraph structure should show you is that—regardless of how many (or how few) sub-points you introduce—you must discuss *each* sub-point in its own paragraph and offer facts, examples, etc; consequently, you may have a four-, five-, six-, or seven-paragraph essay.

If you introduce a sub-point that you cannot develop as fully as the rest, then revise your essay and eliminate that sub-point.

Make Yours Better!

Note that the basic lack of Organization in this essay makes it difficult to read and follow.

■ The first paragraph tells us the main idea of the essay and clearly sets up the order of the essay.

■ The second paragraph follows the pattern laid out by the introduction in a very predictable way. The supporting information the author uses, however, is not clearly linked to fluorine.

■ This paragraph jumps from the main idea of fluorine in nuclear science to very specific supporting details with no transition.

■ The connection between fluoride and fluorine should be made here, not in the introduction. As in previous paragraphs, better transitions are needed to link the main idea and the supporting details. The conclusion sentence is vague and simplistic.

Fluorine is both an extremely dangerous element and a highly useful tool. It is the most reactive of all the elements in the periodic table, combining with elements that usually do not combine. It is also extremely poisonous and can cause very severe burns.

On the other hand, it can be very helpful to scientists working on household products, projects related to nuclear science, and dental treatments (in the ionic form called fluoride).

Fluorine is a key element in many household products, including light bulbs, nonstick cooking pans, air conditioners, and refrigerators. The problem is that when the Teflon used on many household products is heated, fumes can be harmful to animals and humans. The Environmental Protection Agency has also found that one of the compounds used to make Teflon may cause cancer.

Fluorine is used in nuclear science to produce uranium, which is an important part of nuclear weapons. Fluorine-18 has a half-life of 110 minutes, so it can be used for positron emission tomography, a kind of scan of the body that results in a 3-D map. This, however, involves injecting radioactive material into a human being, so it can also be dangerous.

Finally, fluoride is used in dental treatments. This is controversial, however, because it may be dangerous. As a result, New Jersey State Assemblyman John V. Kelly would like for fluoridation supplements to be banned in New Jersey, knowing that in 1992, the New Jersey Department of Health released a study linking fluoridated water to bone cancer in young men. Fluoride, however, is very useful for preventing cavities. In fact, many communities add fluoride to drinking water. Just like in all its other uses, fluorine is both very helpful and a possible great danger to mankind.

Essay Critique

The main point of this essay (that fluorine is both useful and dangerous) is clear, and its structure is predictable. In developing the main point, however, the author makes some logical jumps that the reader cannot follow. Better transitions between supporting ideas are needed.

This essay receives a score of 4 on the:

Organization Rubric

8 = There is a strong attempt at an original organizational plan. Minor jumps or gaps are the result of experimenting with a more sophisticated plan.

7 = ADVANCING
The organizational plan shows strong evidence of moving beyond mere formula (e.g. the five-paragraph essay). Jumps or gaps are the result of experimenting with a more sophisticated plan.

6 = The organizational plan of the essay is clear and consistently applied and shows evidence of moving beyond mere formula (e.g. the five-paragraph essay).

5 = The organizational plan of the essay is clear and consistently applied but is obvious and/or formulaic (e.g., the five-paragraph essay), thus limiting the essay's overall effectiveness.

4 = DEVELOPING
An appropriate but obvious organizational plan is apparent and generally followed, but jumps or gaps distract the reader.

Examining the Principles of Organization

How you organize your information is largely your choice as writer, taking into consideration what the subject matter itself demands, and what your intended audience needs. The most common organizational plans you will use are:

Sequential or Chronological Order

A personal narrative or a process essay will probably best be written in sequential, chronological order. A linear thought sequence leading the reader from point A to point D would best be written in sequential order.

> Initially, the children were frightened by the elusive nature of Boo Radley, but as the weeks wore on, they became intrigued by his aloofness and summoned the courage to explore his house. By the end of the summer, they discovered his true greatness through his perfectly-timed act of selflessness.

Modified Chronological Order

A narrative begins with a sequence in chronological order, but interrupts the sequence, where necessary, to explain events or provide information from *before* the first step of the sequence. This interruption and explanation is usually referred to as a flashback.

Some narratives rely on the flashback in order to reveal important background information that is not a part of the main sequence of events or ideas.

> Without thinking, Minerva abruptly swung open the door. For her, acting upon impulse was the norm. When she was a teenager, she had repeatedly heaped herself with trouble because of her spontaneity, smarting off to her parents and teachers. In college, she became esteemed for her quick responses and ability to question the unconfirmed. Now, her impulsive nature seemed to mix with fate at every turn to issue pleasant surprises and good fortune, but this was about to change.

Order of Magnitude or Order of Importance

This type of organization usually begins with the least important fact or least convincing argument, and culminates with the most important or convincing. Appropriate transitions include: *moreover, more importantly,* etc.

Many persuasive or argumentative topics are best discussed by ordering your evidence and examples in terms of their relative importance. Some descriptive essays and definitions also discuss their subject in terms of the relative importance of features or characteristics that help describe or define the subject.

> There were many reasons why Gretchen wanted the glass vase, the priceless Murano glass vase she and Montrose had smuggled home from Venice after their honeymoon. First, it was a thing of beauty; the cobalt blue whispered of moonlight on the Adriatic, while the gold leaf sang of the summer sun. In addition to being beautiful the vase was quite valuable. She choked whenever she thought about the offer she'd received from that collector in California. She would never have another money problem for as long as she lived. But the most important reason of all, the One Reason above All Reasons why she would *not* yield the vase was that Montrose wanted it. It was all he had asked for in their division of property.

Comparison/Contrast

Writing with this organization relies heavily on the purpose of the comparison, whether it is to inform, to persuade, etc. This system of organization also relies heavily on the focus of the comparison:

Subject-by-subject: Describe one item in the comparison fully and then the other. Highlight the points of comparison/contrast in the conclusion.

> The all-popular SUV has experienced positive sales for many years, becoming a family favorite. A vehicle of this type has the necessary space to carry children, their belongings, sports equipment, and still has enough space for the occupants to sit comfortably. Larger engines enable faster pick-up, and improved suspension offers a smoother ride. All of this comes at a price, though, which is painfully evident at the gas pump and in the environment.

To combat the environmental and cost of operation concerns, many automakers have introduced fuel-cell hybrid cars that use as little as one-fourth the amount of gasoline as the large SUV. These vehicles may not sport the same impressive pick-up, but they have otherwise impressive features. The fact that they use significantly less fuel not only means savings at the gas pump, but it also means far fewer pollutants, which is good for the environment. Hybrid cars are amazingly quiet and comfortable, and provide ample headroom and fair cargo space. The IRS has even offered a tax incentive to those who purchase hybrid cars, boosting the cars' appeal and giving the consumer a sense of environmental responsibility. The only major drawback in comparison to the SUV is the noticeable size difference—a family of four might be a bit uncomfortable when the car is also loaded with athletic equipment, and a family of six simply would not find the car practical at all.

Point-by-point: Discuss individual points of comparison, one by one

When choosing a mouth guard for non-helmeted contact sports, athletes used to have one choice—a simple single-sided guard. In the past decade, however, double-sided guards have been developed, the Brain-Pad in particular, to offer greater protection. The Brain-Pad wraps around both the upper and lower teeth to offer double protection, whereas single-sided guards wrap around either the upper or lower teeth, but not both. The Brain-Pad is superior in that it is designed to secure the jaw in a safe position and absorb shock, reducing the risk of concussion caused by jaw impact. Single mouth guards offer no such protection, as they are designed specifically to protect the teeth. The difference is also noticeable in the price: single guards may be purchased for less than one dollar, but the basic Brain-Pad is priced at approximately $9.99.

Descriptions and definitions might use comparison/contrast, as might some persuasive essays in which you want to show the advantages or benefits of one object over another.

Inductive Order

This type of organization leads the reader through a series of particular examples to a general rule or principle. The sequence of ideas progresses as follows:

- first, name an observation (or series of observations)

- then, make an assertion that a pattern exists (based on the observations)

- next, develop a hypothesis to explain the pattern (based on the observations)

- finally, develop a general theory to explain the original observations, as well as similar cases in the future.

> Sally studied for the test and got an A.
> Shoshona studied for the test and got an A.
> Mary studied for the test and got an A.
> Therefore, people who studied for the test got As.

Deductive Order

Writing of this kind begins with a general rule or principle and one or more established facts and follows a train of thought to a logical conclusion. This sequence of ideas progresses as follows:

- first, begin with a theory, or principle

- then, develop a hypothesis concerning specific cases

- next, study those specific cases to test the hypothesis

- finally, confirm the theory.

Principle:	The price of gasoline rises as the demand for gasoline increases.
Fact:	The demand for gasoline increases during the summer when people travel more.
Conclusion:	The price of gasoline increases (will increase) during the summer months.

Note: Deductive Order can also use a general rule or principle to draw conclusions about an unknown or partially known example.

Principle:	The price of gasoline rises as the demand for gasoline increases.
Fact 1:	The demand for gasoline increases during the summer when people travel more.
Fact 2:	The price of gasoline tends to rise during the summer.
Conclusion:	The increase in gasoline prices is attributable to summer travel.

Examining the Effect of Purpose and Mode of Development on Organization

Don't be fooled into believing, however, that choosing an organizational plan is an arbitrary process. The subject matter of the essay and your purpose as a writer will largely dictate to you the types of information you need to include and how best to give that information to your reader.

Consider the six modes of development you learned in the previous book, and look again at the implication of each in selecting an organizational plan:

1. Using **description** to develop an idea implies an awareness of *spatial order,* or *order of magnitude* (from most important to least important or vice versa).

    Development by description is helpful when:
    - informing your reader of something's nature
    - persuading your reader to favor one thing over another
    - expressing an opinion about the quality of something (evaluation)
    - establishing setting or characterization for a piece of fiction, memoir, personal statement, etc.

2. Use of **narration** implies an awareness of *chronological order* (or reverse chronological order).

   Development by narration is most useful when you need to:
   - inform your reader of essential background (what happened before, the history or development of something, etc.)
   - persuade your reader of some future consequence (based on an understanding of past events)
   - tell a story.

   It is still important to note that there are times when you will be strongly tempted to narrate a story's plot, or an author's biography when this information is *not relevant* to your topic. You do not need to summarize an entire novel to discuss the symbolism of a particular image. You do not need to give a step-by-step description of a family vacation to evaluate how that vacation brought you closer to your siblings.

3. The use of **illustration** most likely involves *order of magnitude* (best example to least or vice versa).

   Illustration can be useful when:
   - informing your reader of something's nature by providing examples rather than struggling to describe it
   - persuading your reader how similar (or different) two things are by providing examples of each
   - using an example, especially a simile or metaphor, to express a mood or feeling that is difficult to express in another way
   - creating an entire story as an example of a point you want to establish or a lesson you want to teach your reader.

4. **Process** will almost always imply *chronological order.*

   Process is most helpful when
   - informing your reader how to do something
   - persuading your reader that there is an easier or more efficient way of doing something.

5. The use of **classification** implies *order of magnitude* or possibly *spatial order.*

    Classification is most useful in:
    • informative writing to help your reader understand something in terms of its class or category
    • persuading your reader to view something in a particular way
    • expressing your view of something by the category in which you place it.

6. **Definition** most likely implies *spatial order* or *order of magnitude.*

    Definition is useful when you need to
    • inform your reader of a new term or object or clarify your particular use of a term
    • persuade your reader of the presence (or absence) of some trait (e.g., there is no justice in the court system) by carefully defining what you mean by that trait
    • express your feelings about some abstract concept (love, honor, etc.).

Exercise 1: Determining Purpose and Mode of Development Choosing an Organizational Plan

Based on the nature of the information in each of the following lists, determine the most likely purpose for sharing this information with a reader. Then, state what mode(s) of development would best serve that purpose and identify the most appropriate organizational plan. Explain the reasons for your choices.
Then, in Exercise 2, you will organize the information according to that plan.

1. **List 1—Mall of America**

- over 400 stores
- sometimes called MOA or MoA
- opened in 1992
- more than 40 million visitors a year
- approximately 1,200 employees
- mall with largest total area in the U.S.
- not largest mall in terms of shopping area
- indoor theme park
- plaque in park where home plate used to be
- most-visited shopping mall in the world
- four malls in world have more retail area
- two rollercoasters
- located where Metropolitan Stadium used to be
- anchor stores: Bloomingdale's, Macy's Nordstrom, Sears
- home of Minnesota Vikings and Minnesota Twins
- contains a wedding chapel (Chapel of Love)
- Called a "dinosaur" by *Wall Street Journal* writer several years ago

Purpose:

Mode(s) of Development:

Organizational Plan:

Reasons:

2. List 2—Louis Brandeis

- born in Louisville, Kentucky, on November 13, 1856
- sympathized with trade unions and women's rights causes
- published *Other People's Money* in 1914
- graduated from Harvard in 1877
- published *Business—a Profession* in 1914
- Supreme Court Justice James McReynolds refused to sit next to him at meeting because Brandeis was a Jew
- opposed Espionage Act of World War I
- appointed to the Supreme Court in 1916
- died October 5, 1941
- friend and ally of Supreme Court Justice Oliver Wendell Holmes
- strong supporter of individual rights
- served on Supreme Court until 1939
- first Jew to serve on Supreme Court

Purpose:

Mode(s) of Development:

Organizational Plan:

Reasons:

3. **List 3—Wind Storms**

- tornado = warm, moist air from Gulf of Mexico + cool, dry air from Canada
- are called hurricanes, cyclones, or typhoons, depending on where they occur
- tropical depression = tropical wave developing a swirling motion
- tornadoes need warm, moist air
- hurricanes = Category I (74 mph) – Category V (over 155 mph)
- tornadoes = warm air rises = updraft
- storms that spin around their centers or "eyes" are called "tropical cyclones"
- three types of thunderstorms: single cell, multicell cluster, multicell line or "squall line"
- hurricanes form from a cluster of thunderstorms called "tropical waves"
- tornadoes are typically less than 300 feet wide
- tropical depression = 35 mph maximum sustained winds
- tornadoes = traditional funnel, slender and ropelike, multiple vortices
- most tornadoes track along the ground only a few miles
- favorable conditions for formation of hurricanes = warm water, open sky, away from land
- U.S. hurricanes form off west coast of Africa or in gulf of Mexico
- hurricanes = warm, moist air collides with cooler air, forming updraft
- tropical depression becomes tropical storm at 40 mph winds
- tornadoes = F1 (40-72 mph = doubtful or gale tornado) – F6 (over 319 mph = inconceivable tornado)

Purpose:

Mode(s) of Development:

Organizational Plan:

Reasons:

4. List 4—Bruno Hauptmann's Trial

- Charles Lindbergh testified that the voice of "John" that he heard in the cemetery sounded like the voice of Hauptmann.
- Hauptmann's handwriting had many points of similarity with the ransom notes.
- A murder weapon was never produced as evidence at the trial.
- A section of attic floorboard taken from Hauptmann's apartment precisely matched the grain of wood used for "rail 16" of the ladder found at the kidnap scene.
- Neither Lindbergh nor the go-between who delivered the ransom initially identified Hauptmann as the recipient.
- "Rail 16" had four rare square nail holes that matched the nails used in Hauptmann's attic.
- Fingerprints from the crime scene were never presented as evidence at the trial.
- Hauptmann had a criminal record in Germany, including a conviction that involved a second-story job using a ladder.
- No one saw Hauptmann climb into Lindbergh's second-story window.
- Hauptmann quit his job immediately after the ransom was paid.
- Violet Sharpe, the Lindberghs' maid, was unable to identify the man she had gone to a roadhouse with the night of the kidnapping.
- On discovering that his son was missing, Charles Lindbergh called his lawyer before calling the police.
- At least one witness testified to seeing Hauptmann around the Lindbergh estate on two occasions before the kidnapping.
- Charles Lindbergh discovered the ransom note sitting on the windowsill when he was alone in the nursery.
- A taxi driver testified that the man who gave him a note to deliver to Dr. Condon, the man who delivered the ransom money, was Hauptmann.
- No one saw Hauptmann with the baby.
- A movie theater cashier identified Hauptmann as having passed a marked $10 gold certificate.
- Hauptmann refused an offer of $90,000.00 from a Hearst newspaper for his public "confession."
- Both Hauptmann's handwriting and the handwriting on the ransom notes had backward "N"s and unclosed "o"s.
- Police failed to measure footprints found near the Lindbergh home.
- Both Hauptmann's handwriting sample and the ransom notes had the same shaped "t"s, and the same curls to the "y"s.

- Hauptmann misspelled many of the same words that were misspelled in the ransom notes.
- The ladder contained over 400 sets of prints, yet none belonged to Hauptmann.
- Both Hauptmann and the author of the ransom notes misspelled "where" as "were," "our" as "ouer," "later" as "latter," "signature" as "signuture," and "boat" as "boad."
- Dr. John Condon, the man who delivered the ransom money to a man named "John" in a dark cemetery, testified that "John" resembled Bruno Hauptmann.
- Dr. Condon's phone number was found written on a closet wall in Hauptmann's kitchen.
- The length of the badly decomposed body found two miles from the Lindbergh home was measured at its autopsy as 33 inches.
- The Lindbergh's dog did not bark the night of the kidnapping.
- A gas station attendant identified Hauptmann as having passed a marked $10 gold certificate.
- $14,000 in ransom money was found in a tin can hidden in Hauptmann's garage.
- Violet Sharpe, the Lindberghs' maid, could not give the names of the other couple who had accompanied her and her date to a roadhouse on the night of the kidnapping.
- Prosecutors failed to provide the defense with evidence that might have suggested Hauptmann's innocence.
- The baby's length was advertised on widely-distributed posters as 29 inches.
- Initial FBI reports suggested that the kidnapping required two persons.
- At the trial, Charles Lindbergh was unable to remember where he had been during the day of his son's disappearance.
- Violet Sharpe, Lindbergh's maid, committed suicide after police identified her as a suspect.
- Hauptmann continued to assert his innocence all the way to the electric chair.
- After the trial, a reporter admitted to writing Dr. Condon's phone number on a closet wall in Hauptmann's kitchen.
- One popular theory suggests that Lindbergh's sister-in-law, Elizabeth Morrow, killed her nephew in a jealous rage over having been spurned by Lindbergh.
- Not a single footprint or fingerprint, at the Hopewell house, belonged to Hauptmann.

- Anne Morrow Lindbergh and the household staff testified that their dog always barked at strangers.
- Neither Anne Morrow Lindbergh nor her sister Elizabeth saw the ransom note during their initial search of the nursery.

Purpose:

Mode(s) of Development:

Organizational Plan:

Reasons:

5. List 5—Batman as Anti-hero

- Rampant crime and corruption in Gotham City indicate normal police function is not effective in Gotham.
- Bruce Wayne is haunted by deaths of parents.
- "black knight" of medieval lore = evil knight (opposite of knight in shining armor)
- Bruce Wayne has unlimited financial resources.
- Batman works with commissioner but does not cooperate with police in general.
- anti-hero lacks courage, honesty, or grace
- anti-hero often weak and/or confused
- anti-hero's character reflects modern society's ambivalence toward traditional moral and social values
- Batman is fully human.
- anti-hero is amoral, neither good nor bad
- Bats are nocturnal creatures.
- Batman's methods are often violent.
- Dark Knight = pun for "dark night"
- anti-hero sides with good due to circumstances.
- Batman's hideout is a cave, not fortress, mountains, or citadel.
- anti-hero motivated by fear, desire for vengeance, etc.
- bats typically associated with evil; frightening (vampires, etc.).
- anti-hero's actions are ethically questionable, even borderline illegal.
- anti-hero is not always sympathetic or likeable character.
- Batman's nickname = Dark Knight
- typical anti-hero has secret or tragedy in past.
- Batman is snot from supernatural origins.

Purpose:

Mode(s) of Development:

Organizational Plan:

Reasons:

Exercise 2: Writing and Using Outlines

Using the details from Exercise 1, write an outline for each list. Follow the organizational plans that you chose in Exercise 1.

Remember the format of the formal, academic outline:

Each level of develpoment is significant because:

- Roman numerals (I, II, III) are the main ideas you want to establish in your essay.
  - Upper case letters (A, B, C) are the sub-points into which you can divide your main ideas.
    - Arabic numerals (1, 2, 3) are supporting details.
      - Lower case letters (a, b, c) are explanations of details.
        - And so on.

✓ *DIFFERENT ITEMS AT THE SAME LEVEL OF DEVELOPMENT ARE INDENTED EQUALLY.*

✓ *YOU CANNOT HAVE ONLY ONE ITEM AT A PARTICULAR LEVEL.*

✓ *DEVELOP EVERY PART OF YOUR TOPIC TO THE SAME LEVEL.*

1. **List 1—Mall of America**
   Outline:

2. **List 2—Louis Brandeis**
   Outline:

3. List 3—Wind Storms
   Outline:

4. List 4—Bruno Hauptmann's Trial
   Outline:

5. List 5—Batman as Anti-hero
   Outline:

Exercise 3: Writing an Essay from an Outline

Choose one of the outlines you wrote for Exercise 2, and write an essay based on your outline.

Exercise 4: Using Your Outline to Diagnose Problems in Your Essay

Examine the draft of the essay you wrote and decide:

- *do you need any additional information?*

- *do you have too much information?*

- *how can you improve the organizational plan or your division of ideas into main ideas, sub-points, and supporting details?*

Describe any changes you would make to the outline in order to write a better draft.

Exercise 5: Assessing Your Outline and Organizational Plan

Examine each of the outlines you wrote in Exercise 2 and decide:

- do you need any additional information?

- do you have too much information?

- how can you improve the organizational plan or your division of ideas into main ideas, sub-points, and supporting details?

Describe any changes you would make to the outline. (NOTE: You do not have to critique and revise the outline you used in Exercises 3 and 4.)

1. List 1—Mall of America

2. List 2—Louis Brandeis

3. List 3—Wind Storms

4. List 4—Bruno Hauptmann's Trial

5. List 5—Batman as Anti-hero

Exercise 6: Outlining an Essay

Outline the "Make Yours Better" essay on page 36. Remember that your Roman numerals represent main points of development not individual paragraphs.

- *Copy each line from your outline onto index cards without the outline notation.*

- *Rearrange the cards and experiment with different orderings and groupings.*

- *After you have arrived at the ordering and grouping of ideas that you think will make the most effective essay, re-write the essay.*

- *Write a few brief, informal paragraphs about why the grouping/ordering you chose is more effective than the original order.*

Exercise 7: Drafting an Outline from Notes

1. *Look again at the notes you took on the Christopher Columbus passage in Trait One. It might be helpful to reread the passage before you review your notes, and possibly take additional notes as you find more pertinent information or discover new insights.*

2. *Considering your thesis and notes, draft an outline.*

3. *Organize your cards into the order of your outline and write the first draft of your essay.*

   (NOTE: With a good thesis statement, your outline will reflect more than a mere summary/repeat of the article).

Writing Opportunity: *The Homework Essay: Analyzing a Reading*

A t the Novice level, you learned how to write a book review as a way to show what you had learned in independent reading. Another important way to discuss something you have read is to analyze it. Analysis is very different from reporting, evaluating, and even interpreting. While interpretation asserts *what* a selection might mean, analysis looks more closely at *how* the author has constructed the selection to convey its meaning to the audience.

Many upper-level high school courses and college courses require you to analyze poetry, fiction, editorials, television and print advertisements, and many other messages. As you learn to analyze how other writers work, you will be able to apply some of their techniques to your own writing.

Organization is an important trait in an analysis because you will be taking the selection you are analyzing apart and discussing the individual parts in an order that will not confuse your reader.

Apply the techniques you learned in this chapter to create an organizational plan that will clearly establish a focus for your reader and help him or her follow your train of thought.

Step 1: *Choose your topic*
What are you going to analyze? Make certain you know the selection's full title and genre, as well as the author's full and correct name.

Step 2: *Draft your thesis*

Read the selection you have chosen (or been assigned) to analyze. Make certain you have an understanding of the author's main point, and then examine the passage's tone, organization plan, sentence structure, word choice, etc. In other words, apply the traits you have been studying and practicing in this series to understand how the author of your passage constructed his or her work.

Then, as you did in Trait One, Exercise 1, write a single sentence that states the overall meaning of the selection you are analyzing and suggests the supporting points.

Example:

President Lyndon Baines Johnson, in his 1964 State of the Union Address, employs linear, sequential thinking, straightforward language—only slightly tinged with sentimentalism—and a respectful, almost conciliatory, tone to evoke compassion in the members of Congress and garner support for his Great Society.

Time Clue: Let's assume you have a week to write your analysis. You should read the passage—even the first time— paying as much attention to how it's written as to what it means. Reading the passage, probably several times, taking the appropriate notes, and developing a thesis statement should take your first two days.

Step 3: *Think about the characteristics of the passage and jot them down to begin your outline*

Here, you will examine how the author of your passage uses the six essential traits you are learning when you write: *development and elaboration, organization, sentence structure and variety, word choice, conventions,* and *voice.* Your analysis will discuss how each of these traits functions in the selection to create the effect and convey the information your author intends.

As you did with your book review in the previous book, jot down your points on index cards and experiment with different orders.

Flip through the passage and write down the specific details that explain, support, and illustrate your claims about the author's technique.

Write these also on index cards.

Time Clue: For a weeklong assignment, you can safely devote one or two days to this step. Remember that it will be better for you to have too much material at this point than too little. You can always edit out the details that you don't need.

Hint: If you have trouble finding examples of a trait, then that is probably a good sign that the trait is not really present. Drop it from your thesis and your outline. You will probably need to replace it with a trait you *can* support with examples.

Step 4: *Write your first draft*
Make it as good as you can. This is more than a freewrite because you have already found your examples and organized them into a logical order. This should take only as much time as it takes your hands to physically write or type it.

Time Clue: Less than one day.

Step 5: *Revise and rewrite*
Set your draft aside for at least a day so that you can look at it with fresh eyes in order to revise it effectively. Remember that—for a weeklong assignment—you need to build into your schedule a day when you will not work on the assignment.

Then, read your draft and look for holes in the information and gaps in the structure and organizational plan. Are you being absolutely clear? Are you offering specific details from the book to illustrate your point and support your claims? You also want to pay attention to grammar, mechanics, spelling, and so on.

If you have time, give your revised draft to another person to read and critique.

Finally, create a new, clean draft of the paper.

Time Clue: You have just one day left for this step, but if you've been careful thinking, planning, and drafting all along, this is plenty of time.

Step 6: *Turn in your analysis*

Trait Three
Sentence Structure and Variety

Composing Powerful Sentences

D EVELOPING WRITERS have essentially mastered the basic grammatical unit of the sentence. They are able to communicate correctly and clearly with an audience. By mastering a variety of sentence structures, the developing writer will be able to communicate even more clearly and effectively.

Sentence variety is a means by which the writer helps the audience to understand what ideas are most important, what ideas support or explain other ideas, etc. Variety of sentence structures also contribute to style and voice, as the way sentences are organized affects the message communicated.

Make Yours Better!

Note that incorrect sentence structure and a lack of sentence variety make this otherwise interesting and informative essay very difficult to read.

The wife of the Italian revolutionary Giuseppe Garibaldi had many experiences; modern women would find them amazing or horrifying. Born Ana Maria de Jesus Ribeiro da Silva in 1821, she was part of a family of poor fishermen and herders, native to the state of Santa Caterina, an island in the southern part of Brazil. As it was becoming independent from Portugal, in fact, a year after she was born, civil war was in store for Brazil and many other countries in South America. It was the Age of Revolutions, which, along with her own independent spirit, guaranteed that Ana would have a life that was not ordinary.

Marrying her first husband in 1835, Ana left him to join Giuseppe Garibaldi, on the ship the Rio Pardo. In 1839, in southern Brazil, fighting for a separatist republic, Garibaldi, an Italian later called the "Hero of Two Worlds," had become a hero to many. In 1841, to help in its war against Argentina, the couple moved to Uruguay; the dictator, whose name was Juan Manuel de Rosas, was attempting to take back Uruguay and Paraguay as provinces of Argentina. Ana helped her husband and took care of the

■ The writer of this passage is experimenting with longer, more complex sentences; however, some of the sentences go on too long with descriptive phrases.

■ The writer also needs to be careful using pronouns ("it," "them,"); in longer sentences, it is hard to keep track of the antecedent.

■ The writer uses good, vivid details to keep the reader's interest.

■ The paragraph is confusing, however, because the details are forced together to make longer sentences, even when they have no relation to one another.

family; they would have four children. When the youngest, Minotti, was only twelve days old, with Minotti in a piece of cloth slung around her neck, Ana was crossing deserts without food and leading her horse across raging rivers. She got malaria; when Giuseppe was given nine hundred cattle, she helped herd them six hundred miles.

Giuseppe went back to Italy to fight in the revolutions there; defending the Roman Republic against the French who tried to restore the Papal state, he was joined by Ana. She, in 1849, pregnant with their fifth child, died of illness. Bringing to an end a long, exciting life, her death was not the end of their love for her husband Giuseppe; he, it is said, always wore a scarf of hers when he went into battle, even long after she died.

Essay Critique

This essay has plenty of detail, but its sentences are awkwardly structured and confuse the reader. The student's urge to use complex sentences is good, but he or she needs to make sure that these sentences contribute to the reader's understanding. One way to avoid some of these problems is by reading the passage aloud to someone else.

This essay receives a score of 4 on the:

Sentence Structure Rubric

8 = **There is evidence of** an awareness of audience, purpose, tone, and the demands of the topic in sentence structure choices. Minor lapses in tone and style—on the sentence level—weaken the overall effect.

7 = **ADVANCING**
The writer has made intentional sentence formation choices for the sake of clarity and impact, but the resulting tone and voice are not fully appropriate to the audience, purpose, and topic. Minor problems in structure, grammar, and/or word choice make the essay less effective than it might be.

6 = **The writer has made** a concerted effort to use a variety of structures to enhance the effectiveness of the essay. Sentences are clear, but minor problems resulting from an attempt to use more sophisticated structures detract from the overall effectiveness of the essay.

5 = **There is an attempt** to vary sentence length and structure, but it appears to be variety for variety's sake rather than topic, purpose, audience, and voice determining appropriate sentence structure. Minor problems in structure, grammar, and/or word choice make them less effective than they might be. These errors can be corrected with minor revision (insertion of words, creation of appositives and/or subordinate clauses, etc.).

4 = **DEVELOPING**
There is evidence of experimentation with sentence variety, but this variety is forced and may result in awkward and inappropriate constructions.

63

Combining Simple Sentences Using Appositives

An appositive is a noun, noun phrase, or relative clause that provides additional information about the subject or another noun in the sentence. Frequently, in paragraphs with many simple sentences, two or more of the sentences can be combined by using an appositive. To form an appositive, simply put the noun or noun phrase that is "in apposition" right after the noun it is explaining.

Note that appositives are usually separated from the rest of the sentence by commas.

1. Albert Einstein developed the theory of relativity.

2. Albert Einstein was a leading figure in the World Government Movement.

Revised as one sentence with an appositive:

Albert Einstein, a leading figure in the World Government Movement, developed the theory of relativity.

Why Use Appositives in Your Writing?

1. Appositives make your writing concise.
   A good rule of thumb is never to use two sentences to say what you can say in one. As the example shows, you can include both pieces of information—that Albert Einstein was a leader in the World Government Movement, and that he developed the theory of relativity—in the same sentence.

2. Appositives help indicate what information is "most important."
   The more important information (the information being clarified by the appositive) is always in the main clause of the sentence; the less important information is in the appositive.

   If your main point above were that Albert Einstein was a leader in the World Government Movement, your sentence would read: "Albert Einstein, the developer of the theory of relativity, was a leading figure in the World Government Movement."

Note, however, that even though the information in the appositive is "less important," it must still be relevant to the main point of the passage. If it is not relevant, leave it out altogether.

3. Appositives help add variety to the length and structure of your sentences. Using a variety of sentence structures makes your writing more interesting for others to read.

    It will also show a stronger command of the conventions of standard written English when your writing is scored by a scale similar to the one in Appendix One.

    This will improve your score on important writing tests like the SAT and your state's writing assessment.

Exercise 1: Using Appositives to Combine Sentences

Combine the two sentences in each pair using an appositive. Remember that you are saying the information in the appositive is "less important" than the information in the main part of the sentence. You should separate the appositive from the rest of the sentence with commas.

1. Our pitcher was George Hiller.
    George won over twenty games.

    Revised Sentence:

2. Ms. Winters is our math teacher.
    She won a $50,000 science foundation research grant.

    Revised Sentence:

3. Ashua Contiki is a security guard in the City.
Last night, he arrested someone for armed robbery.

Revised Sentence:

4. Gertrude Caroline Ederle was the first woman to successfully swim across the English Channel.
She completed the feat on August 30th, 1926, in 14 hours and 39 minutes.

Revised Sentence:

5. Crispus Attucks was the first American slain during the Revolutionary War. He was a black man who was leading a group of colonists in a riot against the British in Boston.

Revised Sentence:

6. Now write five of your own sentences. Have fun. Be creative. Make certain, however, that every sentence has an appositive that provides additional and relevant information about the noun it follows.

a.

b.

c.

d.

e.

Combining Simple Sentences Using Compound Subjects, Predicates, and Objects

Many developing writers offer their readers a long string of short and choppy sentences because they don't think to write a sentence with a compound subject or compound predicate. Note the following sentences.

When we visited New York City, we went to the Empire State Building. We also went to a play. And we took a carriage ride through Central Park.

Revised with a compound predicate:

When we visited New York City, we went to the Empire State Building, saw a play, and took a carriage ride through Central Park.

Alejandro and Momar did not go to New York with the class. Neither did Susannah. Jon did not go either.

Revised with a compound subject:

Alejandro, Momar, Susannah, and Jon did not go to New York with the class.

Exercise 2: Combining Sentences Using Compound Components

Combine each group of sentences by forming compound subjects, predicates, or objects. Remember that compound subjects act like plural subjects in a sentence. Use correct capitalization and end punctuation.

1. My brother is a scoutmaster.
My father is a scoutmaster.
My uncle is a scoutmaster.

Revised Sentence:

2. We sat at the table.
We drank our coffee.
We ate our cereal.
Then, we left for work.

Revised Sentence:

3. My brother is not any good in math.
My sister always did poorly in math.
And my mother said that she always got bad grades in math too.

Revised Sentence:

4. Before you leave, rake the lawn.
Then, cut the lawn with the mower.
And then put out the trash.

Revised Sentence:

5. Larry ran out of his house.
He tripped over his bicycle.
He sprained his ankle.

Revised Sentence:

6. Now write five original sentences with compound subjects and five sentences with compound predicates.

a.

b.

c.

d.

e.

Compound Sentences: Combining Simple Sentences Using Coordinating Conjunctions

Another way to avoid an uninteresting string of simple sentences is to combine closely-related sentences into compound sentences using a coordinating conjunction, such as "and," "but," or "or." Remember, however, that creating a compound sentence with a coordinating conjunction tells your reader that the two combined ideas are equal in importance and very closely related in meaning.

Note that there is a comma before the coordinating conjunction in a compound sentence.

We asked our mother politely. She said we could go to the dance.

Revised: *We asked our mother politely, and she said we could go to the dance.*

Monique said she would drive us in her car. She was called suddenly into work.

Revised: *Monique said she would drive us in her car, but she was called suddenly into work.*

Do you want to go on the bus? Should I try to get someone else to drive us?

Revised: *Do you want to go on the bus, or should I try to get someone else to drive us?*

Why Use Compound Sentences in Your Writing?

1. Compound sentences help the reader understand the relative importance of the information.

    Combining two ideas into one compound sentence will establish two things for your reader:

    - the two ideas are very closely related (so closely related that they belong in the same sentence);

    - both ideas in the sentence are equally important; both are equal parts of the main idea.

2. The coordinating conjunction in the compound sentence establishes the relationship between the two combined ideas.

    - **And** joins two similar ideas together: *Artemis drove the car,* **and** *Diana read the road map.*

    - **But** joins two contrasting ideas: *Diana wanted to drive,* **but** *she did not know how to operate a manual transmission.*

    - **Or** joins two alternative ideas: *Will Diana learn how to drive a stick shift,* **or** *will she be stuck reading maps for the rest of her life?*

    - **Nor** joins two negative alternative ideas: *Outright failure is not an option,* **nor** *should you settle for anything less than an absolute victory.*

      It is possible to use *nor* without a preceding negative element, but it is unusual and almost excessively formal: *I am thoroughly convinced of Ivan's qualifications for this job,* **nor** *do I question his integrity.*

    - **So** shows that the second idea is the result of the first: *The weather report threatened rain,* **so** *we decided to keep the convertible top closed.*

      Be careful with the conjunction **so**. When it is used to establish a cause and effect relationship as in the above example, the compound sentence is punctuated with a comma.

      If, however, the **so** is being used to mean "as well" or "in addition," then the first main clause is followed by a semicolon: *Christianity is not the only monotheistic religion;* **so** *are Judaism and Islam.*

- **For** introduces the reason for the preceding clause, but it implies a before-and-after time sequence more strongly than using "because" or "since" do: *The guests were happy to have a seat in the shade, for it had been a long, dusty journey on the coach.*

  For is also more formal—almost literary—than "because" or "since."

- **Yet** introduces an idea or event that happens despite the occurrence in the first clause. *The snow fell steadily, yet Jim was able to make it to the cabin on time.*

3. Well-constructed compound sentences help add variety to the length and structure of your sentences.
Having a variety of sentence structures available to you makes your writing more interesting for others to read.

It will also show a stronger command of the conventions of standard written English when your writing is scored by a scale similar to the one at the beginning of this book.

This will improve your score on important writing tests like the SAT and your state's writing assessment.

Exercise 3: Using Coordinating Conjunctions Correctly: AND, BUT, OR

Combine each group of sentences into a compound sentence using "and," "but," or "or" as your coordinating conjunction.

You should be able to guess from the pair of sentences which conjunction is most appropriate. Explain why you chose the conjunction you did.

Make certain you use correct internal and end punctuation and capitalization.

1. The rain was extremely heavy last night.
The seedlings we planted are all right.

Revised Sentence:

Explanation:

2. We can repair the old car.
We can buy a new one.

Revised Sentence:

Explanation:

3. The new building will not be ready until June.
We weren't going to move in until July anyway.

Revised Sentence:

Explanation:

4. Sahara applied to MIT.
They offered her a full, four-year scholarship.

Revised Sentence:

Explanation:

5. You can give me what I want now.
I can scream and kick until you give in.

Revised Sentence:

Explanation:

Exercise 4: Using Coordinating Conjunctions Correctly: NOR, SO, FOR

Combine each group of sentences into a compound sentence using "nor," "so," or "for" as your coordinating conjunctions.

You should be able to guess from the pair of sentences which conjunction is most appropriate. Explain why you chose the conjunction you did.

Make certain you use correct internal and end punctuation and capitalization.

1. I will not entertain your question.
I will not tolerate any further interruptions.

Revised Sentence:

Explanation:

2. Dryope cut a flower sacred to the goddess Lotus.
Lotus turned her into a tree.

Revised Sentence:

Explanation:

3. We must seek shelter immediately.
The night is falling fast.

Revised Sentence:

Explanation:

4. Nikko wanted to open his own restaurant.
He took a combination of cooking and business courses in school.

Revised Sentence:

Explanation:

5. The connection between reading and success in school is well established.
Many schools are increasing the amount their students must read.

Revised Sentence:

Explanation:

6. I have serious doubts about that firm's ability to do the job.
I do not like how they handle their clients.

Revised Sentence:

Explanation:

7. The boss was genuinely sorry to let the employee go.
He liked the young woman and felt she did a good job.

Revised Sentence:

Explanation:

8. Mr. Carson did not have time to cover the entire chapter before the test.
He expected the students to know the material anyway.

Revised Sentence:

Explanation:

9. Now write ten original compound sentences. Make certain that you use each
of the seven coordinating conjunctions at least once.

a.

b.

c.

d.

e.

f.

g.

h.

i.

j.

Complex Sentences: Combining Simple Sentences Using Subordinate Conjunctions

Subordinate conjunctions bring a variety of relationships to the sentence:
>time
>cause
>condition
>place
>contradiction, etc.

One event happened...
>*...because another happened,*
>*...before another, after another,*
>*...where another happened,*
>*...while another was happening, etc.*

The subordinate clause gives your reader important additional information about the event taking place in the main clause.

Look up the word "subordinate" in the dictionary. Write the definition here:

As the definition of "subordinate" suggests, the material in the subordinate clause of a complex sentence is secondary or supplementary to the material in the main clause. As a writer, you need to know which information is of primary importance to your reader, which information supports that main information, and how to convey that relationship to your reader.

Compare the following two pairs of sentences:

1. Alphonso quit the team, and we lost the state championship.
   We lost the state championship, and Alphonoso quit the team.

2. We lost the state championship **because** Alphonso quit the team.
   Because Alphonso quit the team, we lost the state championship.

Both versions of sentence one are compound sentences like the ones we worked with earlier in this chapter. Both sentences make the information that Alphonso quit the team equal in importance to our losing the state championship. They also make the exact relationship between the two events unclear. In the first version, the reader might infer that we lost the championship *after* Alphonso quit (but the sentence does not allow the reader to conclude that we lost *because* Alphonso quit). The second sentence suggests that Alphonzo quit after we lost. Thus, in this case, using a coordinating conjunction to create a compound sentence does not really help to communicate clearly and completely.

Both sentences in the second pair are complex sentences. Each sentence establishes the main idea that we lost the state championship and then adds that the reason we lost the game was that Alphonso quit the team. Both sentences more clearly communicate this relationship between the two ideas than either sentence in the first pair.

Notice also that, grammatically, the sentence "We lost the state championship" can stand alone as a sentence. This is the main idea of the sentence. "Because Alphonso quit the team" cannot stand alone and is extra information added to explain the main idea. If you were using sentence one in a newspaper article, the headline might read "We Lose State Championship." It would *not* read, "Alphonso Quits Team."

Why Use Complex Sentences in Your Writing?

1. Complex sentences establish the relative importance of the information even more strongly than compound sentences.

2. The subordinating conjunction in the complex sentence establishes the relationship between the two combined ideas.

3. Well-constructed complex sentences help add variety to the length and structure of your sentences.

Having a variety of sentence structures available to you makes your writing more interesting for others to read. Using various structures appropriately will also show a stronger command of the conventions of standard written English when your writing is scored by a scale similar to the one at the beginning of this book. Consequently, this will improve your score on important writing tests like the SAT and your state's writing assessment.

Commonly Used Subordinate Conjunctions

after	before	or else	whereas
although	because	providing	when
as	even if	since	whenever
as if	even	than	where
as long as	though	though	wherever
as soon as	if	unless	whether
as though	in case	until	while
	lest		

Note that, if the subordinate clause introduces the sentence, it is followed by a comma. If the main clause comes first, there is no comma between the main and subordinate clauses.

As
1. because: *As he had only the one bag, check-in did not take long.*
2. when: *We watched sadly as his plane took off.*

After
1. later in time: *After the plane took off, we went home.*

Although, though, even though
1. in spite of the fact that:
   Although there was a lot of traffic, we made good time.
   We made good time even though there was a lot of traffic.

As though, as if
1. like, seeming similar to (usually introduces the subjunctive, "if contrary to fact"; **see** page 144:

   He looked as though he'd seen a ghost.
   She acts as if she were the Queen of Sheba.

Note: While *as if* and *as though* mean the same thing as *like,* they are conjunctions while *like* is a preposition. It is grammatically incorrect to use *like* to introduce a subordinate clause:

> **Incorrect:** He looks *like* he's lost his best friend.
>
> **Correct:** He looks *as if* he's lost his best friend.

Before
1. earlier than:

   Why do stores put up their Christmas decorations before Halloween has passed?
   Before you leave, Fifi will show you her new trick.

Because
1. for the reason that: *I couldn't go to the party because I lost my invitation.*

If
1. on condition that: *If I get another ticket, my insurance company will cancel my policy.*

Do not confuse the *conditional,* as in the above example, with the *subjunctive* (see page 144). The conditional establishes the consequences of a condition that might actually exist. The speaker above might get another ticket, and the consequence of that would be losing his insurance. The subjunctive establishes the consequences of conditions that do not and will not ever exist: "*If* I *were* King of the World, I'd end all poverty."

Lest

1. for fear that: *The surgeon was especially careful, lest he remove the wrong organ.*

Note: the use of the *subjunctive mood* in the clause with **lest**. This indicates that the action in the first clause is intended to make the consequence in the second clause impossible.

Providing or provided

1. on condition that, a stronger alternative to "if" that sets up a clearer cause-and-effect relationship between the subordinate and the main clauses: *You should recover from your flu in no time, provided you follow all of your doctor's instructions.*

Since

1. from a past time: *She has taught here at Randolph High since she graduated from college.*

2. because: *Since she has seniority over everyone else, she gets to emcee at the awards assembly.*

Note: Many careless writers confuse *since* with *sense*.

Than

1. used in comparisons: *Marquette is a better dancer than you are.*

Note: Many careless writers confuse *than* with *then*.

Note: Often the verb following *than* is understood. The sentence, "Abraham is better at mathematics than Isaac," actually means "Abraham is better at mathematics than Isaac *is*."

Because *than* can also be used as a preposition, you will want to be very careful to indicate what exactly you mean in your comparison.

Consider the sentence: *I love you more than Sarah.*
Does that mean: *I love you more than Sarah (does)?*
or: *I love you more than (I love) Sarah?*

Both are equally possible, and it is your job as writer to make your meaning clear to your reader.

Unless

1. except on the condition that, almost the negative of "if": *Unless you study, you will not pass the exam.*

Until

1. up to the time when, before:
   I will wait until I hear from you.
   We will not leave until you've settled down.

2. to the extent that: *We ran until we couldn't run any more.*

Whereas

1. because: *Whereas this land is reserved for public use, you cannot demand that I leave.*

Note: *Whereas* is a very formal, almost archaic, word. It is now heard almost exclusively in formal proclamations, in the clauses that establish the reasons for the proclamation.

When

1. at or during the time that: *When the bell rings, the class begins.*

Whenever

1. at any or every time that: *My eyes get watery whenever I see someone else cry.*

Where

1. at or in the place that: *Place that package where the other packages are.*

Wherever

1. at or in any or every place that: *Li told her employer that she was willing to live wherever there was a job for her.*

Note: Questions that begin with *when, whenever, where,* or *wherever* are not subordinate clauses.

Whether

1. regardless of which alternative is: *I can't tell from the tone of the letter whether she's angry or not.*

Note: *Whether* does not mean the same thing as *if*, and the two words are not interchangeable. *If* indicates a single condition (*if* it rains...) while *whether* always carries with it the sense of two alternatives (*whether...or not*), even if the second alternative is left unstated (*It's not clear* **whether** *the party is still on.*)

While

1. during the time when: *While Rome burned, Nero played his violin.*

2. although: *While I can't speak for Roger, I do think I understand what he's feeling.*

The following phrases are also often used at the beginning of subordinate clauses:

As long as

1. if: *As long as I have to go, I may as well enjoy myself.*

2. while: *He has been secretary of that organization for as long as I have been a member.*

As soon as

1. immediately when: *Call me as soon as you get there.*

Even if

1. in spite of a possibility: *We will go to their party even if we have to walk there.*

In case

1. because of a possibility: *We'll take our transit card in case the subways are running.*

Or else

1. otherwise: *You must listen carefully or else you won't know what to do.*

Exercise 5: Combining Ideas Using Complex Sentences

Each of the following sets contains two simple sentences. Combine these two sentences into one complex sentence. You may move words around and drop or add words. Be careful to use subordinating, not coordinating, conjunctions.

Then, explain why you chose to subordinate the clause you did, and why you chose the subordinating conjunction you used.

For example:

It was late in the evening. We took the train.

Revision: *Because it was late in the evening, we took the train.*

Explanation: *The main idea of the two sentences is that we took the train; the fact that it was raining is the supplemental information that supplies the reason.*

The clothes were dry in the morning. It had rained some time during the night.

Revision: *The clothes were dry in the morning although it had rained some time during the night.*

Explanation: *The main point—the "announcement"—of this sentence is a sort of surprise that the clothes were dry. The information that it had rained during the night is the additional information that makes the fact of the dry clothes surprising.*

1. The party was disappointing. The promised "celebrity entertainment" turned out to be a juggling chimpanzee.

Revision:

Explanation:

2. Everybody laughed. The chimp dropped all the balls he was juggling.

Revision:

Explanation:

3. I will go tomorrow. I may take you.

Revision:

Explanation:

4. I did not know the answer. The teacher asked someone else.

Revision:

Explanation:

5. John and Phillia were late. They still caught the train.

Revision:

Explanation:

6. I bought a new car. The price of the car was right. I need a new car for my job.

Revision:

Explanation:

7. Some people get upset. These people eat chocolate ice cream.

Revision:

Explanation:

8. The toddler was afraid of monsters in his closet. He would not go to bed.

Revision:

Explanation:

9. Sebastian is learning to cook. He might have a dinner party.

Revision:

Explanation:

10. We read outdated magazines and tried to sleep. We waited for our mother in the doctor's office.

Revision:

Explanation:

11. Justin couldn't handle a lasso. Justin wanted the role of the cowboy in the play.

Revision:

Explanation:

12. I happen to see Barbara many places. She is always happy and whistling.

Revision:

Explanation:

13. Janine and I disagree strongly on many issues. We are still good friends.

Revision:

Explanation:

14. Roberto complained that he hadn't had a really good ice cream sundae in a long time. The last time he had a really good ice cream sundae was when his girlfriend Roberta worked at the Smoothie-Shake.

Revision:

Explanation:

15. The dean handed the graduates their diplomas. At the same time, he shook hands with them.

Revision:

Explanation:

16. Write five original complex sentences that contain subordinate clauses. Pay close attention to appropriate punctuation and capitalization.

a.

b.

c.

d.

e.

Complex Sentences: Combining Simple Sentences Using Relative Pronouns

Words like "who," "whom," "which," "that," and "whose" can be used as **relative pronouns**. That means they can introduce **relative clauses**, a type of subordinate clause that offers additional information about one of the nouns in the main clause of the sentence.

In the sentence:

Martin Luther King, Jr., **who was assassinated in April of 1968,** was a key figure in the Civil Rights Movement in the United States.

"who was assassinated in April of 1968" is the relative clause, and <u>who</u> is the relative pronoun.

A relative clause—like all subordinate clauses—contains information that is relevant, but not as "important" as the information in the main clause.

Study the following examples, in which sets of simple sentences have been combined into complex sentences, each containing a main clause and a relative clause.

George Washington is called the "Father of our Country." He was our first president.

Revision: *George Washington, <u>who was our first president,</u> is called the "Father of our Country."*

Do you know a person? The person I am looking for owns that car.

Revision: *Do you know <u>who owns that car</u>?*
Do you know <u>whose car that is</u>?

The guru asked the disciple a question. The disciple could not answer the question.

Revision: *The guru asked the disciple a question <u>that the disciple could not answer.</u>*

A few important notes about your writing style:

1. **"Who," "whom," and "whose"** are the relative pronouns used to refer to people. *It is very bad style to use **that** when writing about a person.*

Incorrect: The candidate shook hands with everyone **that** lived in my neighborhood.

Correct: The candidate shook hands with everyone **who** lived in my neighborhood.

2. Relative clauses, like appositives, convey additional, relevant information about a noun in the sentence. Like appositives, they are usually set off from the main clause by commas.

3. **Restrictive** relative clauses, though, are not set off by commas. A **restrictive** relative clause is one that restricts the meaning of the noun it modifies. Compare the two sentences below:

Example 1: My father, who is a gourmet chef, once wanted to be an astronaut.

Example 2: The principal assigned detentions to all students who skipped last period study hall.

In Example 1, the relative clause ("who is a gourmet chef") does not restrict the meaning of "my father" and is not essential to the sentence: "My father once wanted to be an astronaut."

In Example 2, the relative clause ("who skipped last period study hall") *does* restrict the meaning of the sentence. The principal did not assign detention to all students, only "all students who skipped last period study hall." This is an example of a restrictive relative clause, and is *not* set off from the main clause by commas.

Most grammarians insist that clauses beginning with the word *that* must be restrictive relative clauses. When a restrictive clause refers to a person, it must begin with the word *who* or *whom.*

Learn to differentiate between restrictive and non-restrictive relative clauses.

All the students, who loved the principal, sent him birthday cards.

All the students who loved the principal sent him birthday cards.

Exercise 6: Combining Sentences Using Relative Clauses

Combine the following sentences, embedding one as a subordinate clause beginning with a relative pronoun. Be careful to punctuate each relative clause correctly and use the correct capitalization and punctuation at the end of the sentence. Then, explain why you chose to subordinate the clause that you did.

1. Joe's snakes were kept in a cage. The snakes escaped and one ate his pet rabbit.

Revised sentence:

Explanation:

2. Kelly pitched a perfect game. Kelly pitched for our team.

Revised sentence:

Explanation:

3. John's coat was stolen. He got that coat from his Uncle.

Revised sentence:

Explanation:

4. Christopher Columbus was Italian. Columbus got the money to pay for his trip from Queen Isabella of Spain.

Revised sentence:

Explanation:

5. The barn burned down. The barn belonged to Mr. Katz.

Revised sentence:

Explanation:

6. The boy took the car without permission. He was arrested.

Revised sentence:

Explanation:

7. John bought the picture. He really liked the picture. His brother had painted it.

Revised sentence:

Explanation:

8. The little engine pulled the train full of toys and treats to the children on the other side of the mountain. The little engine could pull the train.

Revised sentence:

Explanation:

9. Some people believe in witches and ghosts. These people are often frightened at night. These people are superstitious.

Revised sentence:

Explanation:

10. Ms. Chumly was my mother's best friend. Ms. Chumly cried the hardest at my mother's funeral.

Revised sentence:

Explanation:

11. The Minstrel Play Company is now a traveling company. They used to have their own theater in the city.

Revised sentence:

Explanation:

12. I like to buy glass marbles. The glass marbles I like to buy are the clear ones with swirls inside.

Revised sentence:

Explanation:

13. Astrid planted her tomato plants. They were smaller than usual.

Revised sentence:

Explanation:

14. Where did you put the calamine lotion? You bought it last year when I had poison ivy.

Revised sentence:

Explanation:

15. We give candy to the children on Halloween. The children have to be wearing Halloween costumes.

Revised sentence:

Explanation:

Writing Compound Sentences and Compound-Complex Sentences

In the last several lessons, we combined two or more simple sentences to form single compound sentences (using a coordinating conjunction), or single complex sentences (using subordinate conjunctions and relative pronouns).

In this next exercise, we will link at least one complex sentence with an additional main clause, creating a **compound-complex sentence.** In other words, we will be joining a compound sentence and one or more complex sentences. The new sentence will contain two independent (main clauses that can stand alone) and one or more dependent clauses (subordinate or relative clauses that cannot stand alone).

For example: I will vote for him. I do not trust him. I think he is dishonest.

Revised: I will vote for him,   **but**   I do not trust him

main/independent clause   *coordinating conjunction*   *main/independent clause*

because I think he is dishonest.

subordinate/dependent clause

Exercise 7: Combining Ideas Using Compound-Complex Sentences

Combine each the following sets of simple sentences into a single compound-complex sentence. Then, explain why you chose to subordinate the information you did.

1. It was raining hard. John's game was canceled. He went to Joan's house.

Revised sentence:

Explanation:

2. I did not have my homework. I did not go to class. I failed the test.

Revised sentence:

Explanation:

3. Mary was late for the party. It had started at nine o'clock. She did not have a good time.

Revised sentence:

Explanation:

4. Monisha and Shayla were best friends. They had known each other since kindergarten. They had all the same interests.

Revised sentence:

Explanation:

5. The costume was rented by someone else. I had wanted that costume. I got to the rental store too late.

Revised sentence:

Explanation:

6. *Write five original compound-complex sentences.*
Pay close attention to appropriate punctuation and capitalization.

a.

b.

c.

d.

e.

NOTE: It is not very important that you remember the terms for each structure, but it is extremely important that you remember the reason for using each structure, how each helps to make your writing clearer, and the appropriate capitalization and punctuation for each structure.

Exercise 8: Revising Sentence Structure

The following passage is not badly written except for inefficient and ineffective use of sentence structures. Revise the passage to make it clearer, a little shorter, and a more pleasant read.

Austin, Nevada, is a small, unincorporated community of approximately 340 residents. It is situated in the geographic center of Nevada. It stands on the western slopes of the Toiyabe Range. U.S. Highway 50 passes right through the town. Highway 50 is known as the "Loneliest Road in America." Austin is a popular spot for tourists to stop and spend the night. It is what is called a "living ghost town." This means that it is still inhabited, but it is not nearly as large as it once was. It is not as bustling a town as it once was either.

The town was originally named for Austin, Texas. Other local history buffs claim they do not know exactly how the town got its name. Austin was founded in 1862. William Talcott discovered a ledge of silver ore. He worked for the Overland Mail and Stage Company. A silver rush followed. The town's population boomed to 10,000 people. This happened within two years.

There is another version of the story. This one says that the silver rush was triggered by a horse. The horse was owned by a W.H. Talbott. The horse kicked up a piece of quartz. This quartz contained gold and silver. It was an accident. Talbott staked out a claim. The silver rush was on. There is a third version of the story. This version claims that a Pony Express horse kicked over a rock. Austin grew quickly. The Nevada Legislature made Austin the county seat. Jacobsville had been the county seat. The county was called Lander County.

The Nevada Central Railroad was built. The railroad was built in 1880. The reason the railroad was built was to connect Austin with the transcontinental railroad. This made it easier to transport the silver out. It also made it easier to bring needed goods in. The book was almost over. Austin's mining activity had reached its peak. This peak had been in the late 1860s. The peak lasted into the early 1870s. The last really strong year for Austin was 1872. In 1872, they produced $250,000 in silver. Major silver production ended completely. This happened in 1887. The Atomic Age dawned in the 1950s. When this happened, uranium deposits were discovered. They were discovered in the area near Austin. The uranium ore in the deposits discovered in the area around Austin proved to be of low quality. Turquoise is mined there. This turquoise is of high quality. There is too small a quantity of turquoise here. That is why it has not spurred a resurrection of Austin. Austin was once a rich and powerful town.

Today, Austin is a quiet town. It has about 340 people. It is the best preserved example of an early Nevada mining town. Perhaps that is true. Many of the original buildings are still standing. They help the town keep its atmosphere. Austin has an intriguing historical atmosphere. The Catholic church was built in 1866. The Methodist church was also built in 1866. The Methodist church is now used as a community center. The Catholic church is called St. Augustine's. It is being restored. When it is finished being restored, it will be used as a cultural center. It will serve Central Nevada. The Episcopal church was built in 1878. Some consider the Episcopal church to be the prettiest frontier church still standing. It is still in regular use. A walk along Austin's street can truly transport one back. You can be transported back to a bygone era. A walk along Austin's streets provides the historian with a rare glimpse. The casual tourist gets a rare glimpse too. They can glimpse what life was like in the past. They can especially see what life was like over a century ago.

Writing Opportunity: *The Homework Essay: Summarizing Contrasting Readings*

At the Novice level, you learned how to write a précis and chapter summary to show what you had learned from independent reading. Summary is neither interpretation nor analysis. While interpretation invites you to explain what you think the passage means (and support your claims with evidence from the passage), and analysis asks you to take the passage apart and explain how it works, summary is an accurate repeat—in your own words—of what the author of the original passage is saying. There is no interpretation, analysis, or evaluation in a good summary.

While summary, then, might appear to be an unimportant and simple process, it is actually quite difficult for a reader not to impose his or her own thoughts and opinions onto another's work. It is often important, however, to be able to report accurately what another has said and done *before* going on to interpretation, analysis, and evaluation. Many upper-level high school courses and college courses will require you to perform research where you look at the writing, experiments, and original thoughts of others and explain them to demonstrate that you understand them. This understanding, then, might be the foundation of further study and thought.

Sentence formation is an especially important trait in a summary because, in a summary, you need to convey a great deal of information—all of the main ideas and the most important development of the passages you're summarizing—in as few words and sentences as possible. Here is where your ability to use compound and complex sentences, appositives, and other structures to communicate the relationships between ideas will be a main factor in determining your summary's success.

Step 1: *Choose your topic*

Find two articles that take opposing positions on a debatable issue (or use two readings assigned by your teacher). Make certain you know the selections' full titles and genre, as well as the authors' full and correct names.

Step 2: *Draft your thesis*

Read the selections you have chosen (or been assigned) to analyze. Make certain you have an understanding of the authors' arguments, and the evidence each presents in support of his or her point. Pay special attention to evidence from one article that directly refutes evidence from the other article.

Then, write a single sentence that states the main ideas of the selections you are summarizing and indicates the primary difference between them.

Example:

When Ruth Helior of *The Minnesauka Bugle* and José Manuela, editor-in-chief of *The Sentinel*, write on the issue of school choice, their views could not be more diametrically opposed.

Time Clue: Reading each passage several times, taking the appropriate notes, and developing a thesis statement might take your first two days.

Step 3: *Draft an outline of each passage*

Instead of outlining your summary, outline each passage. Let Roman numerals indicate each author's main areas of development, and capital letters, Arabic numerals, etc., indicate key examples, facts, arguments, etc.

Time Clue: For a weeklong assignment, you can safely devote one or two days to this step. As always, it is better to have too much material at this point, than too little. You can always edit out the details that you don't need.

Step 4: *Write your first draft*

As always, make it as good as you can. You have already found your examples, and your summary has to follow the order of ideas used by your authors. Composing your first draft should take only as much time as it takes your hands to physically write or type it.

Time Clue: Less than one day.

Step 5: *Revise and rewrite*

Set your draft aside for at least a day so that you can look at it with fresh eyes in order to revise it effectively. This is a crucial step for everything you write except for exam and assessment essays that must be completed in one day. Remember that—for a weeklong assignment—you need to build into your schedule a day when you will not work on the assignment.

Look at your draft. Have you offered complete summaries of both articles? Is your summary as brief as it can be—have you used word choice and sentence structure efficiently to convey as much information in as few words as possible? Have you avoided all interpretation and evaluation? (Be especially careful that you aren't suggesting personal support for one view by subtle shifts in tone.)

If you have time, give your revised draft to a person to read and critique. *This is another important step. Even professional writers have friends or writing groups with whom they share their work before it is finished and submitted for publication.*

Finally, create a new, clean draft of the paper.

Time Clue: You have just one day left for this step, but if you've been careful thinking and planning and drafting all along, this is plenty of time.

Step 6: *Turn in your summary.*

Trait Four
Conventions of
Written English

Making Powerful Language Decisions

REMEMBER THAT our goal is to write using Standard American Edited English. There are, of course, two ways to achieve this language correctness. The first is to be familiar enough with the conventions that you habitually speak and write appropriately for your audience and purpose. The second is to realize that—before you ever submit a final draft to its intended audience—you will proofread and edit the piece, correcting any surface errors that you find. The bottom line is that the final draft of your writing must be free of errors in spelling, punctuation, grammar, etc.

Make Yours Better!

Note that frequent and severe deviations from the Conventions of Written English make this essay extremely difficult to read and understand.

Lester Young was one of the best jazz saxophone players in the twentieth century. It was because of Lester Young that there were movements like bebop. Without Lester Young many of the new forms that were made in modern jazz would not have been made. In addition to being an interesting jazz player he had an interesting life.

He was born in 1909 in Woodville, Mississippi. He came from a musical family. Lester's father Willis Handy Young, was a music teacher. He taught his son violin, drums, and, trumpet. Lester picked up the saxophone at the age of thirteen.

When Lester was still a child the family moved to New Orleans. They toured as a group. But Lester left the family band in 1927. In 1933 he moved to Kansas City, Missouri. He played in the band led by Fletcher Henderson. But the members of this band wanted Young to play just like Coleman Hawkins. Hawkins was the most famous jazz saxophone player of the time. Young needed a change. At the club called the Reno Room Young met the piano player and bandleader Count Basie. Lester Young became a part of Count Basies band.

▥ The writer gives us a good thesis statement, but seems afraid to use language beyond a basic level. The presence of punctuation errors shows that this person is still shaky as a writer.

▥ The language remains vague and simplistic here. Because the writer does not use descriptive words, the subject seems flat, and the essay is dull.

■ **This paragraph contains spelling and punctuation errors. These could be excused, though, if the writer were thorough with word choice and sentence length.**

■ **This information gets the reader's interest, but could be described much more vividly.**

■ **The conclusion is flat, simply repeating statements the writer made previously.**

Hawkins had an "aggressive" style. Lester Young was not considered as good as Hawkins because his style was more relaxed. He ignored the critics. He was an innavator because he developed his own style. He especially came up with innavations in time signature. Other players had kept their solo's in the band's time signature. But Lester Young's solos were independent of the band.

Lester Young met the great jazz singer Billie Holiday in the early 1930s. They met at a jam session. After the session they played together in club's in New York. Holiday called Lester "Prez" after President Franklin Roosevelt. This was to be Young's nickname for life.

In the 1940s Lester Young was drafter into the United States Armed Force. Unlike other white musicians, Young was not allowed to play music in the Army. Instead he had to join the regular armed forces. He was then courtmarshelled for having drugs and for having an affair with a white woman. He was discharged in 1945. In 1959, Lester Young died of alcoholism. Some critics say that the recordings made in the final years of Lesters life are not as good as the ones he made with Basie. Both others feel the recordings are the best of his career. Either way Lester Young was one of the most interesting jazz musicians of his genneration.

Essay Critique

There are a few misspellings and punctuation errors in this passage, but overall, it has few mistakes. Now the writer can try presenting the information with more complex sentences, using more interesting words and phrases, and organizing the information so that the reader's attention is captured. The simplicity of the language and the lack of experimentation (even at the risk of making errors), stifle this essay.

This essay receives a score of **4** on the:

Conventions Rubric

8 = **Infrequent, minor surface errors** suggest the need for careful editing, but do not require any revision in order to correct.

7 = ADVANCING
Infrequent surface errors suggest the need for careful editing and some revision of the essay.

6 = **Infrequent minor surface errors** suggest an attempt to experiment with more sophisticated language. These may distract the reader and require substantial revision of the essay.

5 = **Essay is largely free** of basic surface errors. Errors that do appear (semi-colon, complex subject-verb agreement, etc.) suggest an attempt to experiment with more sophisticated language and may interfere with the reader's understanding, requiring extensive revision.

4 = DEVELOPING
Essay is largely free of basic surface errors (spelling, elementary punctuation, capitalization, etc.), but correctness of language is largely governed by simplicity of language.

Using Colons, Semicolons, and Dashes Confidently

Using the Semicolon (;)

Despite its name, the semicolon is more a "big comma" or a "little period," than a variant of the colon. There are three essential ways in which the semicolon comes in handy.

First Semicolon Rule

Use a semicolon to combine two closely related complete sentences. The key here is that the information in the two sentences must be so closely related that it could be in the same sentence. Do not merely combine any two adjacent sentences with a semicolon.

The following two sentences might not indicate the close relationship between my not feeling well and my decision not to attend Laurie's party:

I am not going to Laurie's party.

I don't feel well enough.

So I can combine them into a single sentence with a semicolon:

I am not going to Laurie's party; I don't feel well enough.

Likewise, to say the following in two sentences really does not make it clear that the second sentence is the reason for, or the illustration of, the general statement made in the first sentence:

John is one of our best packers.

He gets his orders out quickly and correctly.

Combining the two clauses makes this relationship much clearer.

John is one of our best packers; he gets his orders out quickly and correctly.

Avoiding and Correcting Comma Splices and Run-on Sentences

A common mistake among developing writers is to combine sentences like the above ones with a comma or with no punctuation. To combine them with a comma instead of a semicolon is called a "comma splice." It is corrected by simply replacing the comma with a semicolon.

Incorrect: You must invite Shaniqua, she is always the life of the party.

Correct: You must invite Shaniqua; she is always the life of the party.

To combine the two clauses with no punctuation is called a "run-on sentence." Again, it is easily fixed by inserting a semicolon between the two clauses.

Incorrect: I'm not really a doctor I just play one on television.

Correct: I'm not really a doctor; I just play one on television.

To some students, these points may seem trivial, but you should always strive to avoid these types of errors. You certainly should look for and correct these during the proofreading and editing stages of your writing process because test scorers search out these kinds of errors.

Exercise 1: Combining Sentences Using Semicolons

Rewrite each of the following pairs of sentences to form compound sentences containing a semicolon. If you choose not to combine the sentences into one, explain why.

1. Betsy's nephew is building her a new house. That carpenter showed them a photograph.

2. They aren't all running toward the barbershop. Tony is studying in the library.

3. The detectives asked him several questions. They have been interrogating him since late yesterday afternoon.

4. Jack didn't talk. Frank had lied.

5. I had been eating. I was interrupted.

6. Catherine has been crying all afternoon. Andy sent her a message.

7. I wasn't sleeping. I was resting my eyes.

8. Miss Johnson doesn't live near our school. Most teachers prefer to keep their addresses private.

9. I don't swim. I jog.

10. Buddy wasn't here because Ned forgot to pick him up. Buddy was at the barbershop.

Second Semicolon Rule

Use a semicolon between two complete sentences linked with a conjunctive adverb or transitional phrase.

Common Conjunctive Adverbs

accordingly	indeed	otherwise
afterwards	likewise	similarly
also	moreover	so
consequently	nevertheless	still
however	nonetheless	therefore

The following two sentences could be combined with a semicolon:

The semicolon is an important tool for developing a more mature writing style.
Indeed, proper use of the semicolon is one of the signs of a thoughtful and careful writer.

Revision: *The semicolon is an important tool for developing a more mature writing style; indeed, proper use of the semicolon is one of the signs of a thoughtful and careful writer.*

While this combination does not necessarily change the meaning of the two sentences, it does allow for some variety in sentence structure and a more mature writer's voice.

It is important to avoid comma splices and run-on sentences. This can be accomplished by proofreading and correcting.

Exercise 2: Using Semicolons and Conjunctive Adverbs to Combine Sentences

Rewrite each of the following pairs of sentences as a compound sentence using a semicolon and a conjunctive adverb. Then, explain why you have placed the conjunctive adverb where you have.

1. Reynaldo had never learned to swim. He tended to be a very nervous Naval officer.

Revision:

Explanation:

2. The lateness of the hour, the bitter cold weather outside, and the fact that he had a bad cold were all reasons Ebenezer Scrooge did not want to venture out with the Ghost of Christmas Past. He went out anyway.

Revision:

Explanation:

3. You have really made a lot of progress as a writer this year. You will be more than ready to enter the next level next year.

Revision:

Explanation:

4. Inexperienced electricians might severely injure themselves. They need to be very careful.

Revision:

Explanation:

5. I felt comfortable asking Isabel to accompany me. The invitation said, "Mr. Humphrey and guest."

Revision:

Explanation:

6. The new Madison Square Garden was supposed to be a modern architectural marvel. I was sad to see the beautiful and elegant Pennsylvania Station demolished.

Revision:

Explanation:

7. Scrooge knew he had amends to make to many people. He raised Bob Cratchet's salary.

Revision:

Explanation:

8. Alexis took the blame and paid to repair the other driver's car. The accident was not her fault at all.

Revision:

Explanation:

9. The CEO never listened to what his Board of Directors said. He always fell asleep at meetings.

Revision:

Explanation:

10. The desire of the financial investors prevailed, and Pennsylvania Station was torn down. Architects from all over the world protested the demolition of the beautiful *beaux arts* train station.

Revision:

Explanation:

Third Semicolon Rule

Use a semicolon between items in a complicated series or list with commas; the semicolon helps clarify the separation between items.

> **Incorrect:** Because she wanted her holiday dinner to be perfect, Naomi bought olives, both green and black, sweet, white, and yellow potatoes, ingredients for apple, pumpkin, and mince pie, two types of rolls; three hot vegetables, and, of course, the turkey.
>
> Notice that in the example above you cannot tell what are the main items in the series and what are the items-within-the items.
>
> **Correct:** Because she wanted her holiday dinner to be perfect, Naomi bought olives, both green and black; sweet, white, and yellow potatoes; ingredients for apple, pumpkin, and mince pie; two types of rolls; three hot vegetables; and, of course, the turkey.

With the semicolons, the difference between the main items is clear.

- DO NOT use a semicolon to introduce a list (see below).

- DO NOT use a semicolon between main clauses joined by coordinating conjunctions (and, nor, but, or, yet, so). The semicolon indicates a relationship between the two main clauses that is even closer than that indicated by these conjunctions.

- DO NOT use a semicolon between a dependent clause and the rest of the sentence.

Incorrect: No one came to the party; even though she'd sent out over a hundred invitations.

Correct: No one came to the party, even though she'd sent out over a hundred invitations.

Incorrect: Even though she sent out over a hundred invitations; no one came to the party.

Correct: Even though she sent out over a hundred invitations, no one came to the party.

Incorrect: Since the weather was bad, Stanley was sick, and Martha was still grieving for her lost poodle; we decided to cancel the ski trip.

Correct: Since the weather was bad, Stanley was sick, and Martha was still grieving for her lost poodle, we decided to cancel the ski trip.

Exercise 3: Using Semicolons Correctly

In the following sentence, insert commas and semicolons in the appropriate places. Then, explain why you used semicolons where you did.

1. Mark who was engaged to Mary's sister Enid whose brother-in-law was Mary's husband Chanille the sister who dropped out of school to dance in New York and Seth the brother who became rich selling pet rocks all celebrated Thanksgiving with their parents Cyril and Beryl McKnought.

   Explanation:

2. Although it was an express the train stopped in Anaheim California Phoenix and Tucson Arizona Albuquerque New Mexico and El Paso and Houston Texas.

   Explanation:

3. Bruce despaired of ever catching up on his reading since he still had the books that his brother had given him the newspapers he'd stolen from his neighbor and the information his sister and brother-in-law had faxed to him.

   Explanation:

4. Antoine Dominick's son his wife Marcia their sons Marvin and Donatello and Max the family's golden retriever spent a quiet holiday at home.

   Explanation:

Using the colon (:)

Think of the colon as an equal sign. Using a colon correctly is not nearly so impressive as proper use of the semicolon (mostly because so many people misuse the semicolon), but it does come in handy.

The colon has two uses.

First Colon Rule

Use a colon as a formal introduction to a quotation or a list when the introductory statement is a complete sentence.

For example, use a colon to:

- **introduce a quotation.**

The closing lines of Charles Dickens' *A Tale of Two Cities* are among the most famous in English literature: "It is a far, far better thing that I do, than I have ever done; it is a far, far better rest that I go to than I have ever known."

Let's not forget what Mother told us as we left the house: "Make sure you take your umbrellas in case it starts to rain."

Notice that in both of the preceding examples, the quotation is introduced by a complete sentence that actually refers to the quotation that's coming. Notice also how the colon is the "equal sign" between the general reference to the quotation and the actual words of the quotation itself.

• **introduce a textual quotation in a formal paper.**

In his famous lecture, "The Substance of Shakespearean Tragedy," A. C. Bradley describes the overall calamity that contributes to the tragic plot in this way:

The suffering and calamity are, moreover, exceptional. They befall a conspicuous person. They are themselves of some striking kind. They are also, as a rule, unexpected, and contrasted with previous happiness or glory. A tale, for example, of a man slowly worn to death by disease, poverty, little cares, sordid vices, petty persecutions, however piteous or dreadful it might be, would not be tragic in the Shakespearean sense. (8)

Here, the quotation is too long to be incorporated into the body of the sentence and set off with quotation marks. As in the other examples, however, the introductory sentence is a complete sentence and refers to the quotation that will follow. Hence, the colon is still the "equal sign" between the general introduction and the action words of the quotation.

• **introduce a quotation from poetry.**

A single line of poetry is presented like any other short quotation. Two lines can be run into your text with a slash mark, called a solidus, to indicate the end of the first line. The quotation is set off with quotation marks, but it is introduced with a colon.

Robert Frost's famous poem, "Mending Wall," begins with the lines: "Something there is that doesn't love a wall,/That sends the frozen-ground-swell under it."

A quotation three lines or longer is set off like the previous A. C. Bradley quotation. Present the quoted lines exactly as they appear on the original page. There are no quotations marks, but the quotation is introduced with a colon.

> The speaker of "Mending Wall" seems to question the building of barriers and walls:
>
> Before I built a wall I'd ask to know
> What I was walling in or walling out,
> And to whom I was like to give offense.

In both of the preceding examples, notice how the colon follows a complete sentence that explains or refers to the quotation that is about to come and serves as a sort of "equal sign" connecting the introduction and the quotation.

- **introduce a list.**

> There are numerous attractions that a first-time visitor to New York City simply *must* see: the Empire State Building, the Metropolitan Museum of Art, Washington Square Park, and Saint Patrick's Cathedral.

Notice how the colon is the "equal sign" that joins the general statement "numerous attractions" and the list of specific attractions.

Second Colon Rule

Use a colon between two complete sentences if the second explains, illustrates, or somehow restates the information in the first. Note the following examples.

> José had one thought on his mind that morning: He needed to do well on his test in order to pass the course.

> Many teachers must work more than one job in order to make ends meet: Even if they do not "moonlight" during the school year, most find some kind of summer employment to supplement their regular salaries.

> Carolyn couldn't decide who was to blame: Was she responsible for the accident, or was Jamie?

> There is no clear-cut rule about the first word of the clause following the colon: Some grammar texts suggest using a capital letter, while others suggest lower case.

> Amal decided not to go right on to graduate school: He'd received a job offer that he simply could not turn down.

Notice that, in all of the above sentences, the second main clause says essentially the same thing as the first. Also notice that the second main clause is capitalized. There is no clear-cut rule about the first word of the clause following the colon: Some grammar texts suggest using a capital letter, while others suggest lower case. Ask your teacher what he or she prefers. Whether you decide to use upper or lower case, be consistent.

- DO NOT use a colon between a verb and its object:

Incorrect: The three most important factors in real estate are: location, location, location.

Correct: The three most important factors in real estate are location, location, location.

Even though the direct object of the above sentences is a list, the part of the sentence introducing the list is not a main clause, and the list is not formally introduced. The colon in the WRONG example does *not* serve as an equal sign between the first and second parts of the sentence

- DO NOT use a colon between a preposition and its object:

Incorrect: Frantic to find her keys, Allison looked in: her purse, her jacket pocket, and her backpack.

Correct: Frantic to find her keys, Allison looked in her purse, her jacket pocket, and her backpack.

Again, even though the object of the proposition is a list, the clause introducing the list is not a main clause, and the list is not formally introduced. The colon in the WRONG example does *not* serve as an equal sign between the first and second parts of the sentence.

- DO NOT use a colon after *including, such as,* or *for example.* The colon means the same thing as these words and would be redundant.

Incorrect: The Winter Olympics include some of my favorite sports, such as: curling, skeleton, and snowshoeing.

Correct: The Winter Olympics include some of my favorite sports, such as curling, skeleton, and snowshoeing.

Exercise 4: Using Colons Correctly

Insert colons in the appropriate places in the sentences below. Then, explain why you have used the colon as you have, or why you have chosen to leave the sentence as it is.

1. Before we left, our mother gave us her typical warning "Be good. And, if you can't be good, be careful."

Explanation:

2. Good writing is the skillful combination of six essential traits development and elaboration, organization, grammar and mechanics, sentence structure, word choice, and voice.

Explanation:

3. The *Beaux Arts* style of architecture is usually known by its grand scale, use of classical features like columns and colonnades, and the predominance of ornaments like carved urns and balustrades.

Explanation:

4. Most theater critics tend to disagree with Steiner Bassingham's sentiment whoever wants to criticize a writer's work must first write something himself.

Explanation:

5. Henry Wadsworth Longfellow wrote the famous poem that begins with the lines "Listen my children and you shall hear/Of the midnight ride of Paul Revere."

Explanation:

Using the dash (—)

There are four occasions in which you might use a dash.

First Dash Rule

Think of the dash as a stronger—and informal—comma and semicolon. There might be times when—for the sake of voice and tone—a phrase or a clause that you'd normally set off with commas will look and sound stronger set off by dashes instead. The trade-off is that the use of dashes will also make your writing look and sound more casual or conversational. Dashes should, therefore, be used sparingly—if at all—in your most formal writing. Note the following examples.

> Konstantin Malloy, the governor's most trusted and popular advisor, will announce his resignation from office later today.
>
> Konstantin Malloy—the governor's most trusted and popular advisor—will announce his resignation from office later today.
>
> The scandal surrounding Malloy's former business partner, allegations of abuse of power, personal misconduct, and questionable income tax returns, still haunts the administration.
>
> The scandal surrounding Malloy's former business partner—allegations of abuse of power, personal misconduct, and questionable income tax returns— still haunts the administration.

All four of the above examples are correct, but the dashes in numbers 2 and 4 invite the reader to pause and consider the inserted information more strongly than the commas do in examples 1 and 3.

Number 4 is also much clearer than number 3 because the dashes definitely establish that the set-off information is an appositive explaining the scandal and not a list of items in addition to the scandal.

Second Dash Rule

Use a dash to indicate an abrupt shift in thought in a sentence.

Elizabeth—fully recovered from her illness and back to school—turned in her first draft.

Third Dash Rule

Use a dash to insert a full sentence within another sentence.

All of the invited guests—I had not been invited but was accompanying Christine—received hand-printed name cards.

Fourth Dash Rule

Use a dash as an informal introduction to a list of items:

House cats seem to do only three things all day—eat, sleep, and eat again.

- DO NOT use a dash in place of a period.

- DO NOT use the dash as an all-purpose punctuation mark that means you don't have to learn the appropriate use of commas, colons, and semicolons.

Exercise 5: Using Dashes Correctly

Rewrite each of the following sentences, replacing commas and semicolons with dashes where appropriate. Then, explain why you have used dashes where you have—or why you have chosen to leave the sentence as it is.

1. Mayor Goldstein, who was nominated for the Nobel Prize in Literature, the Pulitzer Prize for his exposé on graft and corruption in the organic fertilizer industry, and a Hornen Hardart Humanitarian Award for his tireless efforts to feed the hungry in his community, has offered to sell the movie rights to his life story to the highest bidder.

Sentence:

Explanation

2. Mary, Dan, Jeremy, and Jerry rode the bus, Mary has the better car, but no one wanted to drive, all the way from Seattle, Washington, to Portland, Maine.

Sentence:

Explanation

3. Don't forget to stop at the grocery store and pick up those things I need: a toothbrush, some nail polish, and the latest issue of the bridal magazine.

Sentence:

Explanation

4. The problems that Anastasia and Minerva faced in Chapter Three, the bankruptcy, the tragic deaths of their parents and fiancées in the same horrific fire, the loss of Anastasia's job, and Minerva's frightening diagnosis, made the book seem more a farce than a drama.

Sentence:

Explanation

5. A statue of the goddess Minerva, in Greek mythology, she is called Athena, is perched atop the rotunda dome of the United States Capitol.

Sentence:

Explanation

Use dashes with care.

Remember that dashes are informal and conversational, while semicolons and commas are more formal and academic.

Using the Correct Pronoun Case

The *case* of a pronoun signals the pronoun's use in the sentence: Is the pronoun the subject of the sentence, the direct object, a possessive modifier?

Nominative: Use the nominative case when the pronoun is the subject or the predicate noun of the sentence.

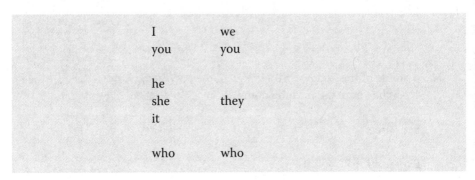

I	we
you	you
he	
she	they
it	
who	who

Possessive: Use the possessive case when the pronoun is a possessive modifier, to show the pronoun's possession of the noun it modifies. Note that nouns form the possessive case by some variant of *'s*, but pronouns do not.

my/mine	our/ours
your/yours	your/yours
his	
her/hers	their/theirs
its	
whose	whose

Note that the possessive of it is its and the possessive of who is whose. There are no apostrophes for either of them.

Objective: Use the objective case when the pronoun is the direct or indirect object of an sentence, or the object of a preposition.

me	us
you	you
him	
her	them
it	
whom	whom

Most of the time, your use of the correct case of the pronoun is by habit. There are a few common errors, however, that may be overlooked in casual, everyday conversation but are inexcusable in formal writing.

Incorrect: *Me and my friend* had a great time last night.

Correction: *My friend and I had a great time last night.*

Explanation: *Me is the objective form of the first person pronoun. As it is the subject of this sentence, the nominative case (I) must be used. I put my friend first (my friend and I not I and my friend) out of simple convention.*

Incorrect: Just *between you and I,* there is a good chance the firm will close after the first of the year.

Correction: *Just between you and me, there is a good chance the firm will close after the first of the year.*

Explanation: *Between is a preposition, and the object of a preposition must be in the objective case.*

Exercise 6: Using Pronoun Case Correctly

Each of the following sentences may contain an error in pronoun case. Correct the error, and then explain why you have made the correction that you have made. If a sentence is correct as it stands, explain why it is correct.

1. As for the first set of papers; they were delivered by a messenger who is faster than me.

Correction:

Explanation:

2. Those flowers were sent to Andrew and I.

Correction:

Explanation:

3. Mary loves Zach more than I.

Correction:

Explanation:

4. Alberto loves Juanita more than me.

Correction:

Explanation:

5. Janice received a larger reward than him.

Correction:

Explanation:

6. Students who have been awarded scholarships pay lower tuition than us.

Correction:

Explanation:

7. Everyone at the game brought their Thermos filled with hot chocolate.

Correction:

Explanation:

8. Alexis and me will go with you and she to the book store.

Correction:

Explanation:

9. Alfonse has a much higher grade point average than me.

Correction:

Explanation:

10. When you call, ask to speak specifically to Daniel or I.

Correction:

Explanation:

11. At the assembly, they announced that Pete and her will be the Homecoming King and Queen.

Correction:

Explanation:

12. My manager and his boss are always arguing; he told me they may never agree.

Correction:

Explanation:

13. The hula dancers greeted my wife and I as we climbed from the plane.

Correction:

Explanation:

14. The portrait certainly did depict the country scene; it was absolutely beautiful.

Correction:

Explanation:

15. Mike, Susan, and I washed the floor ourselves this morning.

Correction:

Explanation:

Who and whom: *Whom* is the objective form of the pronoun *who*. Therefore, *whom* bears the same relationship to *who* as *him* does to *he*. The correct use of *who* and *whom* is really not complicated, but it does take careful thought and attention to the sentences you are writing and the ideas you are communicating. Consider the following examples:

1. Marcia is the person to **whom** the envelope was mailed.

2. She should give the envelope to the person **who** handles that sort of mail.

3. I don't know **who** owns that car.

4. It was hard to tell **whom** the policeman wanted to see.

5. I would hate to guess **who** owes him the money.

6. **Whom** did you invite to the semiformal?

In sentence 1, *whom* is the object of the preposition *to*. The envelope was mailed to *whom*.

In sentence 2, *who* is the subject of the subordinate clause. *Who* handles the mail.

In sentence 3, *who* is again the subject of the subordinate clause. *Who* owns the car.

In sentence 4, *whom* is the direct object of the verb *see* in the subordinate clause. The clause essentially says, *The policeman wanted to see* whom.

In sentence 5, *who* is again the subject of the subordinate clause. The clause reads, *who* owes him money.

In sentence 6, *whom* is the object of the verb *did invite*. Another way of asking the question would be *You did invite whom to the semiformal?*

Exercise 7: Using Who and Whom Correctly

*Fill in the correct form (**who, whom, whoever, whomever**) in the following sentences. Then, explain why you selected the form that you did. Note: The rules for using whoever and whomever are the same as those for who and whom.*

1. _____ scored the winning touchdown?

Explanation:

2. The principal hired _____ for the position?

Explanation:

3. I will give the money to _____ needs it the most.

Explanation:

4. Markus Albright is not only the man _____ wrote the best-selling novel but also the recluse _____ everyone wants to meet.

Explanation:

5. Tasha and _____ will host the next meeting?

Explanation:

6. The student _____ had won the game promised to share his award with _____ had helped him prepare when he returned to school.

Explanation:

7. Jillian entered the room, anxious to catch _____ was passing the secret notes.

Explanation:

8. The school district was broke and could not advertise for the teachers _____ would be the most qualified.

Explanation:

9. Ms. Simmonson is a very hardworking teacher upon _____ the whole department depends.

Explanation:

10. Whether you are punished or not will depend on _____ hears your case.

Explanation:

Using Active Voice and Passive Voice Appropriately

All of the instruction and exercises in this chapter employ your ability to make decisions. The best way to prepare yourself to make these decisions is to understand what your options are, how they work, and which option is more likely to serve your purpose better than another. Remember that your goal is always to write an essay that will communicate clearly and effectively with your reader.

Two of these options are the active versus the passive voices. There are times when you will want to use each, and your choice will work well for you. There will be other times when one or the other will be simply inappropriate.

The key, however, is to understand them both so that—as a writer—you are able to make an intentional choice of which one to use.

Active Voice: In sentences written in **active voice**, the subject *performs* the action expressed in the verb. You probably do most of your writing and speaking in the active voice.

The writer | must decide whether to use the active or passive voice.
subject | *verb*

The writer | must choose | the best arrangement of words.
subject | *verb* | *DO (receiver)*

The best arrangement | communicates | the message most effectively.
subject | *verb* | *DO (receiver)*

Passive Voice: In sentences written in **passive voice**, the subject *receives* the action expressed in the verb; the subject is *acted upon.*

Often, passive voice	is considered formal and academic.
subject (receiver)	verb

Frequently, the performer of the action in the sentence	is not specified.
subject (receiver)	verb

In such a case, the essay	might not be understood	by the reader.
subject (receiver)	verb	performer

Converting Active Voice to Passive Voice

Passive voice is formed by moving the receiver of the action (usually the direct object) to the place of the subject. Then, a form of the verb *to be* is added to the action verb, and the action verb is converted to its past participle form. If the performer of the action is included in the sentence, it appears in a prepositional phrase after the verb.

Active voice:

The oil industry	develops	many new and convenient products.
subject (performer)	verb	DO (receiver)

Passive voice:

Many new and convenient products	are developed	by the oil industry.
subject (receiver)	verb	performer (prep. phrase)

Converting Passive Voice to Active Voice

To change passive voice to active voice, move the performer to the subject, or create a logical performer if there is not one in the sentence. Remove the form of *to be* from the verb, and change the verb to the appropriate tense. Finally, place the receiver in location of the direct object.

Passive voice:

The students │ were told to visit the newly renovated auditorium.
subject (receiver) │ verb

[Note that there is no performer in this sentence, so you need to create one to convert it to active voice.]

Active voice:

The teachers │ told │ the students to visit the newly renovated auditorium.
subject (performer) │ verb │ DO (receiver)

Use passive voice only as required.

Exercise 8: Identifying Active and Passive Voice

Identify whether each of the following sentences is active or passive voice. Then, rewrite all passive sentences as active voice and all active sentences as passive voice. If the performer of the action is not stated in a passive statement, create a logical performer.

Active | Passive   **1.** Mark Twain was born 1835 in Florida, Missouri.

Active | Passive   **2.** In late formative years, Twain moved to Hannibal, Missouri.

Active | Passive   **3.** This area's modern tourism revolves around Twain and the characters of his novels.

Active | Passive   **4.** It is the setting for his most popular novels, *The Adventures of Tom Sawyer* and *Adventures of Huckleberry Finn*.

Active | Passive   **5.** Twain married Olivia Langdon in 1870.

Active | Passive   **6.** Many of Twain's books contained powerful societal messages about racism and the evils of slavery.

Active | Passive   **7.** In some cases, this led to extreme controversy.

Active | Passive   **8.** Many of Twain's books, especially *Huckleberry Finn,* have been banned from schools and libraries across the country.

Active | Passive   **9.** Twain himself was driven off the stage more than once when he appeared to give a speech or a reading of one of his books.

Active | Passive   **10.** *Tom Sawyer* was Mark Twain's first official novel.

Active | Passive   **11.** It was published in 1876.

Active | Passive   **12.** Although it was not as popular as Twain had predicted, it became a classic in American literature by 1910.

Active | Passive   **13.** *Huckleberry Finn* was published in January 1885.

Active | Passive   **14.** Technically, it was the sequel story to *Tom Sawyer*.

Active | Passive   **15.** The book is still considered an American classic.

Unless you know the passive voice is appropriate, you should avoid using it. There are times, however, when the passive voice is the option you must choose as it is the clearest, most correct way to communicate your ideas to your reader. The point is for you to *choose* the passive voice and to *know why* you have made that choice—always keeping in mind what will best serve your audience.

Exercise 9: Deciding When to Use Passive Voice

All of the following sentences are written in the passive voice. Either rewrite the sentence into the active voice or explain why you think it would serve your reader best to keep it in the passive.

1. Many historians believe that the modern age was ushered in by the revolutions that occurred in the United States and France in the eighteenth century.

2. In both revolutions, an aristocratic government was abolished by dissatisfied commoners.

3. In many countries in Europe, especially England, the power of the monarchy had already been limited.

4. In England, the people's rights were represented by Parliament.

5. In the American colonies, the people's rights were denied by the king and Parliament.

6. Medieval and Renaissance views of social class had been challenged by many writers and philosophers of the Enlightenment.

7. In the United States, the idea of human rights is expressed in the Declaration of Independence.

8. These rights are then established in the Bill of Rights.

9. In France, peasants were treated very harshly by the aristocracy and monarchy.

10. The dissatisfaction of the peasants was fueled by harsh weather and famine.

11. The French bourgeoisie were also denied access to political power, even though they had vast economic resources.

12. The former fortress and prison known as the Bastille was stormed by the peasants of Paris on July 14, 1789.

13. This day is still celebrated as Bastille Day.

14. The French Revolution is often considered to be a "failed" revolution because it resulted in the restoration to the throne of the same royal family that had been in power before.

15. Nevertheless, several national revolutions—including the Russian Revolution in the early twentieth century—were inspired by the French Revolution.

Using the Subjunctive Mood

As a developing writer, you will sometimes have to discuss not only what is *real* in the past, present, and future, but also what is *possible* or *conditional*, or what *might have been* true, but isn't. For these times, you will want to be familiar with the SUBJUNCTIVE MOOD.

1. Use the subjunctive mood to establish conditions that are not factual. This is often called "if contrary to fact."

If Carlotta *were* here, she *would cut* the pie into more even slices.

If Carlotta *had come,* she *would have made* the party a lot more fun.

It is clear from the way these sentences are constructed that Carlotta is *not* at the party. She *was not* at the party, and she is *not expected* to be at the party. The possibility of her being there is theoretical, and is contrary to the actual facts.

Notice that the present tense subjunctive mood uses "were," followed by "would." To say "If Carlotta *was* here..." in this case would be incorrect.

An "if contrary to fact" condition in the past is indicated with the past perfect tense.

Remember that the subjunctive mood is used *only* when the condition *is not, was not, and probably will not ever be* true.

2. Use the subjunctive mood to voice a suggestion, request, demand, or warning.

Suggestion:
It *would* be best *that* he *stay* home and study.
Don recommended *that* you *join* the committee.
I suggest *that* you *be* a little quieter.

Request:
Is it essential *that* we *be* there?
The Dean asked *that* Marcia *submit* the final draft of her research paper before the start of vacation.
I propose *that* we *take* the back roads and avoid the traffic on the highway.

Demand:
The teacher insists *that* her students not *bring* food to class.
The boss insisted *that* Maurice not *be* late any more.

Warning:
The doctor's order is *that* he *drink* three large glasses of orange juice a day.
Justin insisted *that* Sharon not *take* the job without first getting a written contract.
It is important *that* you *be standing* there when he gets off the plane.
It is crucial *that* a car *be waiting* for the speaker when her commencement address is over.

Each of the above examples indicates a condition that is not true at the time but might be true in the future.

Less experienced writers sometimes use the conditional (could, should, or would) to express the subjunctive idea of a condition contrary to the facts. While these expressions may be acceptable in informal conversation and writing, they are not acceptable for formal, academic writing.

CONDITIONAL: **I wish he *would be* kinder to me.**

SUBJUNCTIVE: **I wish he *were* kinder to me.**

The **conditional** above is a wish for a possible future improvement in "his" kindness. The **subjunctive** wishes that "his" present level of kindness were already higher (while acknowledging that it isn't).

Exercise 10: Using the Subjunctive Mood Correctly

Some of the sentences below incorrectly use the subjunctive mood. Others are correct because their meaning is not one of the subjunctive uses. Correct the incorrect sentences. Then, for each sentence, explain either why you made the changes you did or why you left the sentence as it is.

1. If I was able to have any car I wanted, I would choose a Mercedes.

Correction:

Explanation:

2. If it is raining when I get there, I'll wait for you in the lobby.

Correction:

Explanation:

3. I waited outside, but if it would have been raining, I would have waited inside.

Correction:

Explanation:

4. After his medical exam, it is very important that Dustin pays close attention to the doctor's instructions.

Correction:

Explanation:

5. The counselor strongly recommends that Monique goes to school every day.

Correction:

Explanation:

6. It would be nice if Bruce were more reliable about his chores.

Correction:

Explanation:

7. I wonder whether it would be possible for penguins to learn how to fly.

Correction:

Explanation:

8. Cincinnatus would have been a Roman dictator for life if he would have been more power-hungry.

Correction:

Explanation:

9. If I was late this morning, it was only because I didn't hear my alarm.

Correction:

Explanation:

10. If I am ever late again, I will be fired.

Correction:

Explanation:

Be careful to use the right mood.

If I were done with my homework, I would be skiing right now.

Exercise 11: Editing Passages

Each of the following passages contains errors, both in the usage covered in this chapter and in basic grammar, mechanics, and spelling. Rewrite each of the paragraphs, correcting the errors. Then, explain your corrections. You do not need to explain corrections involving blatant spelling or grammatical errors.

1. Passage One

Some 60 miles north of New York City on the east banks of the majestic Hudson River is the city of Beacon. When the City of Beacon was incorporated in 1913. It was named by it's founders for its most predominate local landmark—Mount Beacon. While Mount Beacon enjoyed historical significance during the Revolutionary war, as the site of signal fires, lit to warn Revolutionary soldiers of the movements of the British in the region— hence the name Mount *Beacon*—it was a lucertive business partnership at the turn of the Twentieth Century that put Mount Beacon and the town that was named after it on the map.

In 1900, several business men from the towns of Fishkill Landing and Mateawan (the two towns that would be incorporated into the City of Beacon) formed the Incline Railway Association. Each member of the associateion contributed their fair share of start-up funds, and supplied the names of people who, they belived, might lend them money for the project. There goal was to build a Cable Railway to the top of Mount Beacon, eventually this railway would come to be called "The Eighth Wonder of the World," and would hold the record of the world's steepest inclined railway in the world. The railway itself was built by the Otis Elevator Company of Yonkers—on a grade of 65 percent to a height of 1,150 feet above the River. It was opened on Memorial Day 1902, and carried over 1,000 ridders on that first day: a total of 60,000 passengers rode the railway during its first season.

After passengers rode to the summit of the mountain, they were free to entertain themselves at a casino, a restaurant, and a dance hall. A verdana offered a remarkible view of the Hudson River; and coin-operated telescopes allowed tourists to see as far as seventy-five miles away. The adventuresome tourist could hike a mountain path to the D.A.R.'s Mount Beacon Monument built to commemorate the cite of the Revolutionary War signal fires. This was the highest point on the Mountain: and whomever made the trek was treated to a view even more spectaclar then the one from the casino.

The Beaconcrest Hotel also stood at the top and was a popular resort. Unfortunately, the hotel was destroyed by a fire in 1932 and was never rebuilt. Eventually, the casino also burned to the groud. As did the dance hall. If there would have been a water or tower of some kind of firefighting equiptment at the top of the mountain, than maybe the buildings would have been saved.

Even after the fires—however—, the Eight Wonder of the World: the World's Steepest Incline Railway continued to take passengers to the top of Mt. Beacon until fire and vandalism destroyed the trolly station at the foot of the Mountain and one of the two cars. Efforts have been underway sence the late 1990's to restore the incline railway; and work has actually begun with the design and construction of the Gateway Park at the foot of the mountain.

If the railway was rebuilt, than maybe they would also rebuild a restaurant at the Top. These tourist attractions were enjoyed by many thousands of people in the Past, and it would be nice if they could enjoy them again.

That is the gaol of the Mount Beacon Incline Railway Restoration Society. Perhaps in the not-too-distant future, passengers will once again ride up the Worlds Steepest Incline Railway and marvel at the view from the summit of historic Mount Beacon.

Revision:

Explanation(s):

2. Passage Two

The city of Milwaukee, Wisconcon, began as a pair of rival trading posts on the West Shore of what is now Lake Michigan. From the time the earliest French settlers—mostly trappers and fur traders—arrived in the area, it was called "Milwaukee." Local historians say the name came from a word in the language of the the the Potawotami Tribe: Mahn-ah-wauk, which meant "council grounds." In the first written mention of a word at all similar to Milwaukee, a British officer stationed in Green Bay in 1761, a Lieutenant James Gorrell, wrote the name of the area as Milwacky. Earlier in 1697, Father Zenobe Membre, whom was traveling with the French explorer LaSalle, wrote about a river called: Mellioke.

In 1818, Solomon Juneau came to the Milwaukee area to work as an assistant to Jacques Vieau at Vieau's trading post. A few years later, Juneau married Vieau's daughter; and essentially took over the trading post. A wealthy Green Bay lawyer and businessman, Morgan Martin saw the potential for town development on the site of Juneau's trading post. If he was to be able to develop the land, however, he would need Juneaus coperation, because the trader held the rights to the land east of the Milwaukee River. He asked Juneau to enter into a business partnership with him. If Junea thought there were a chance to continue trading beaver pelts successfully, the City might never have developed. But beaver were growing scarce in the area, and Juneau realized that the days of the fur trade were nearly over. He accepted Martin's proposal, and the town that sprang up on the site of Juneau's former trading post came to be know as Juneautown.

Byron Kilbourn was an unscrupulous businessman from Ohio, who saw the potential for a port city on the Milwaukee River. Because Juneau controlled the rights to the land east of the river, Kilbourn had to set his sights on the west. This land technically belonged to the Potawatomi Indians. In a plot with an unethical surveyor, Kilbourn had this land included on an 1835 federal survey. The Potawatomi were given permission to remain on the land for three years. When this time was up, they were rounded up by federal officials and led west of the Mississippi. Kilbourn was then able to take control of the area which he developed as Kilbourntown, a separate community from Juneautown.

By the 1840s, an intense rivalry between the east side (Juneautown) and the west side (Kilbourntown) had developed largely because Kilbourn tried to isolate the east, making it essentially a satellite of Kilbourntown. In 1840, the Wisconsin Legislature required the rival communities to build a drawbridge to replace the inefficient and antiquated ferry system. Kilbourn and the west siders saw the bridge as a threat to their autonomy.

The tension reached its climax in May of 1845 when Kilbourn's supporters caused the west end of the bridge to collapse into the river. An east side mob gathered at the river. This time, violence was avoided, but two weeks later, an east side group destroyed two smaller bridges in an attempt to cut the west side off from the south and the east. A skirmish broke out between the West and East. Several people were seriously injured. After the situation calmed down, Milwaukeeans on both sides of the river realized that they would have to learn how to coperate and live as one community. After all, if the rivalry was allowed to continue, both sides might loose in the long run. The following year, West and East joined to become the City of Milwaukee. A City Charter was adopted, and Solomon Juneau—not Byron Kilbourn—was elected the first mayor.

Revision:

Explanation(s):

Writing Opportunity: *The Homework Essay: Arguing the Point*

Probably the most important type of writing you'll do in high school and college—and arguably the most exciting—is argumentative or persuasive writing. In fact, argumentation is the basis of most of the Greek philosopher Aristotle's work on rhetoric.

One of the most convenient ways to talk about persuasion is to think about a criminal trial—especially from the standpoint of the prosecution. You've probably seen enough crime-drama-police-courtroom television shows and movies to know that the investigators gather evidence from which they draw a conclusion—Suspect A is guilty.

Tthe "burden of proof" is on the prosecution. The prosecutors must prove to the jury that Suspect A is guilty. If they do not have enough evidence, or if they do not demonstrate that their interpretation of the evidence is accurate, then Suspect A is declared not guilty.

Consider how the trial runs. The prosecuting attorneys assert to the jury that Suspect A is guilty. (This is the thesis.) They then list the pieces of evidence they will present and the witnesses and experts who will be called to testify. That is the introduction.

Then, each piece of evidence is displayed, and its relevance is discussed. Each witness and expert is called to testify. This is the body of the argument.

Finally, the prosecution sums up, for the jury, the evidence and the witnesses' and experts' testimony. The prosecution then calls for the jury to agree with its initial thesis that Suspect A is guilty. This is the conclusion.

Effective use of language conventions is an important trait in argumentation because—as you learned in the chapter—the placement of a comma or semicolon, or the difference in meaning between the subjunctive and conditional can make the difference between convincing your reader of the validity of your argument or looking foolish.

Step 1: *Choose your topic*

Choose a debatable issue about which you have some knowledge and have an opinion you know you can defend with facts, not just emotional appeal.

Take a stand on the issue, and defend your position to a general audience of intelligent but skeptical readers. If you need more information, track it down in the library or on the Internet; in a paper of this length (one or two pages), however, you should use secondary sources sparingly.

Step 2: *Draft your thesis*

In a single sentence, state your view on the issue you have chosen and suggest the primary reason for that view.

Example:

Because the benefits to be gained for those who suffer from congenital handicaps and debilitating neurological diseases far outweighs any risk to viable human life, Congress should not place any restrictions on the medical community's conducting stem-cell research.

Time Clue: This is a short step, as you already know something about your issue and already have an opinion.

Hint: Notice how the sample thesis does *not* use the first person. Even though your opinion is the basis of this essay, it is *not necessary* (in fact, it is actually bad form and reduces your credibility) to use statements like, "In my opinion," "I feel," "I believe."

Step 3: *Brainstorm and gather your evidence and support*
List every fact or case study you know to support your thesis. Make certain you rely only on factual evidence and reasonable support. A good argument is never based on emotional appeals and sentiment.

Try to anticipate the arguments of those who disagree with you and attempt to refute them—or at least explain why they are less convincing than your own arguments.

If you need to, read an article or two on your issue and take notes on information these sources offer in support of your thesis. Be certain you keep all of the bibliographic information you will need to cite every "outside" source you use.

Time Clue: Since you invested so little time in the thesis stage, you can safely devote one or two days to this step—possibly even three if you have to look for outside information. As always, it is better to have too much material at this point than too little. You don't have to use every bit of evidence you've collected, but you cannot use evidence you do not have.

Step 4: *Write your outline*
As you organize your ideas to draft your outline, you will have to take several important factors into consideration:
- How much about your topic does your reader already know?
- How much background information will you have to give before beginning your argument?
- Given the evidence and support you have collected, what are your main areas of development?
- What is the best order in which to present your evidence? Is chronological order appropriate? From most important to least important? From least to most important?
- Will the basic five-paragraph essay format work for you, or is it too narrow to allow you to present whatever background you need plus all of the evidence you have?

Additionally, as you organize your thoughts and plan your outline, try to avoid common mistakes in reasoning. (See Appendix 2)

It never hurts to try out two or three different versions of your outline. This is where copying over the points and bits of evidence onto index cards comes in handy.

Also, remember to use your outline—as you did in the previous book—to diagnose potential problems with your essay: points of discussion that are under-developed, overdeveloped, etc. Now is the time to fix them.

Time Clue: Give yourself a day. Again, now is not when you come up with your ideas since you already have them. What you're doing here is organizing them.

Step 5: *Write your first draft(s)*

As always, make it as good as you can. (You have already found your examples, and your summary has to follow the order of ideas explained in your evidence.) Composing your first draft should take only as much time as it takes your hands to write or type it physically.

If you quote from any sources or use information from a source that is not common knowledge, cite it with an MLA in-text citation and include the source in a list of works cited at the end of the paper. (See Appendix Three)

If you drafted more than one version of your outline, write a first draft for each. You can decide later which is the one you want to revise and submit.

Time Clue: Less than one day.

Step 6: *Revise and rewrite*

Set your drafts aside for at least a day so that you can look at them with fresh eyes in order to choose the one that is most effective and revise that one effectively.

Remember that—for a weeklong assignment—you need to build into your schedule a day when you will not work on the assignment.

When you consider which draft to revise and then begin to revise that one, ask yourself the following:

- Have you offered enough (but not too much) background information?
- Do you have enough evidence to convince someone who is inclined not to agree with you?
- Is your evidence factual and objective or do you rely on emotional appeals and sentimentalism?
- Is your evidence presented in a logical order so that you are leading your reader to accept your conclusion as reasonable and valid?

If you have time, give your revised draft to another person to read and critique. This is another important step. Even professional writers have friends or writing groups with whom they share their work before it is finished submitted for publication.

Finally, create a new, clean draft of the paper.

> **Time Clue:** You have just one day left for this step, but if you have carefully thought, planned, and drafted all along, this is plenty of time.

Step 7: *Turn in your argumentative essay.*

3 SIMPLE TRUTHS AND 6 ESSENTIAL TRAITS OF POWERFUL WRITING

Applying
the
Third Truth

Powerful writing is painless to read.

3
Simple Truths
and

6
Essential Traits
of

Powerful Writing

Facial see FACE

Fiddle see FAIR

Facsimile see COPY 2

Factor see COMPONENT

Fad see CRAZE

Fade see DIM

Fan see ENTHUSIAST

Faint see WEAK

Fair 1. Fair, unbiased, just, impartial, equitable: free from suspicion or favoritism for any particular side of an issue

FAIR is characterized by frankness, honesty, and an absence of prejudice—said of persons, character, or conduct; as, a fair man; fair dealing; a fair statement. "I would call it *fair* play." —William Shakespeare. *ant.* unfair, dishonest, prejudiced

UNBIASED is characterized by the absolute absence of prejudice in considering a situation. "The lawyers search for *unbiased* jurors." *ant.* biased, partial, partisan

JUST indicates a sense of righteousness, decency, and virtue when acting and making decisions. "The parties awaited a *just* resolution from the arbitrator." *ant.* unjust, unfair, undeserved

IMPARTIAL indicates complete fairness and an absence of favoritism for any party in making a decision. "Our justice system ensures that the judge will be *impartial* when deciding a sentence." *ant.* partial, prejudiced, one-sided

EQUITABLE stresses fairness and equal treatment. "Our Constitution emphasizes *equitable* treatment of all citizens under the law." *ant.* inequitable, undue, unfair, unbalanced

Trait Five

Word Choice

TRAIT FIVE:
WORD CHOICE

Make Yours Better!

Note that ineffective Word Choice impairs the effectiveness of this otherwise decent essay.

In the Democratic Republic of the Congo, in the heart of the Virunga Mountains, the volcano called Mount Nyiragongo rises with truly great power. It is not a dormant volcano, but an active volcano that may erupt at any time. In fact, it is a common belief that when this volcano does erupt, great loss of life and destruction of property will almost certainly be the result.

The Virunga Mountains are a part of the Great Rift Valley, a vastly large geographical formation stretching all the way from Mozambique to the country of Syria; the Valley is caused by the separation of three different tectonic plates: the Arabian plate, Nubian plate, and Somalian plate. Where there is a space between plates, the earth is unstable, and earthquakes often take place. Also, lava can come up through the earth, causing a volcano to erupt. Mount Nyiragongo itself is actually straddling two of the African plates that are breaking apart from each other.

Mount Nyiragongo has a main crater that is about 800 feet in depth and 3200 feet in width, which sometimes is filled up with a lake of boiling-hot lava. In fact, this is the world's very largest lake of lava. The lava in this lake is especially dangerous in the event of an eruption because it has a very low silica content. This means that the lava flows at an incredibly fast speed. The lightning-fast speed of Nyiragongo's lava, combined with the steepness of the mountain itself, means that the lava can bury surrounding villages in almost no time at all.

Along with another monster volcano, Nyamiragura, Nyiragongo has caused almost half of the volcanic eruptions that have ever occurred upon the continent of Africa. In the terrible 1977 eruption of Nyiragongo, at least seventy people, and possibly many more, lost their lives. In the 2002 eruption, many people were evacuated in time, but all the same, at least forty people perished. Because of the very fluid lava moving at a breakneck

- The author of the passage has good information and a clear thesis statement, but uses some clichés and "filler" phrases like "in fact." Even if a lot of words were removed from this paragraph, it could still convey the same information.

- Several words and phrases could be removed from this paragraph.

- The writer could make the passage vivid and exciting for the reader by choosing very specific details and arranging them carefully, rather than being repetitive and overusing words like "very" and trite phrases like "lightning-fast."

pace, there was not much time to get away. In addition to the disastrous death toll, hundreds of thousands of people suffered the loss of their homes.

Another lava lake, a sign of impending disaster, has now formed in the gargantuan crater of Mount Nyiragongo. This lake is being observed carefully by concerned scientists, because it may signal that another tragic eruption of the volcano is soon to take place.

Essay Critique

While there is a conscious effort to make the essay dramatic, the writer tends to depend on exaggerated adjectives and unnecessary phrases ("in fact," "almost certainly"). The extra words quickly tire the reader. Instead of using exaggerated language, the writer could make the passage exciting through strong, specific detail and original organization of information.

This essay receives a score of **4** on the:

Word Choice Rubric

8 = **For the most part**, the writer has chosen vivid, powerful nouns and verbs, but still relies somewhat on obviously unfamiliar words from vocabulary lists and thesauri. Figurative devices (similes, metaphors, allusions) are original, but inappropriate to the other aspects of the essay (subject, occasion, audience, purpose).

7 = ADVANCING
Attempts at vividness might result in strained or forced usage – "thesaurus-itis". Use of figurative language (similes, metaphors, allusions) is experimental and therefore might be unoriginal, out-of-place, or forced.

6 = **Word choice is at** times vivid and strong, but occasionally lapses into the weak and general. The essay may exhibit signs of "thesaurus-itis:" words appear straight from the pages of Roget, but do not quite fit, are not used quite appropriately. The use of figurative language (similes, metaphors, allusions) is experimental and therefore might be unoriginal, out-of-place, or forced.

5 = **Word choice shows strong** attempts at vividness, but vague and inexact language predominates. Figurative language (similes, metaphors, allusions) is unoriginal, and does not really contribute to the overall effect of the essay.

4 = DEVELOPING
Attempts at vividness are more frequent and intentional, but miss the mark, often resulting in clichès, awkward constructions, and an overuse of adjective-noun and adverb-verb phrases, especially overuse of amplifiers like "very," "truly," etc.

161

Exercise 1: Finding Specific Words

Using a thesaurus and/or dictionary, find two synonyms for each of the following words or phrases. In some cases, the synonyms will not be "stronger" than the word below, but they will indicate a different, more specific use. Use each of the synonyms in a sentence. After the sentence, write a brief explanation of why you chose that synonym for that sentence.

For example:

average: *statistical norm or mean; common*

Sentence: *The mean temperature for Juneau, Alaska, for the past thirty years is 25.7°F.*

Explanation: *(Mean is defined simply as "the mathematical average.")*

Sentence: *Neither political party seems really to represent the needs of the common citizen.*

Explanation: *(The definition of common is "ordinary" or "normal.")*

1. relative:

Sentence:

Explanation:

Sentence:

Explanation:

2. deal with:

Sentence:

Explanation:

Sentence:

Explanation:

3. get:

Sentence:

Explanation:

Sentence:

Explanation:

6. modern:

Sentence:

Explanation:

Sentence:

Explanation:

4. pretty:

Sentence:

Explanation:

Sentence:

Explanation:

7. fashionable:

Sentence:

Explanation:

Sentence:

Explanation:

5. fair:

Sentence:

Explanation:

Sentence:

Explanation:

8. good:

Sentence:

Explanation:

Sentence:

Explanation:

9. bad:

Sentence:

Explanation:

Sentence:

Explanation:

10. happy:

Sentence:

Explanation:

Sentence:

Explanation:

11. large:

Sentence:

Explanation:

Sentence:

Explanation:

12. small:

Sentence:

Explanation:

Sentence:

Explanation:

13. ability:

Sentence:

Explanation:

Sentence:

Explanation:

14. communicate:

Sentence:

Explanation:

Sentence:

Explanation:

15. institution:

Sentence:

Explanation:

Sentence:

Explanation:

18. alternative:

Sentence:

Explanation:

Sentence:

Explanation:

16. idea:

Sentence:

Explanation:

Sentence:

Explanation:

19. interface:

Sentence:

Explanation:

Sentence:

Explanation:

17. situation:

Sentence:

Explanation:

Sentence:

Explanation:

20. overcrowded:

Sentence:

Explanation:

Sentence:

Explanation:

Working Toward Conciseness

A common problem in American English is the tendency to waste words, using phrases of two, three, or more words where one well-chosen word would suffice.

Overuse of the word "very" is only one of the ways writers of American English waste words. Often, the excess wordage is the result of redundancy or simply applying a common convention in an inappropriate way.

The first paragraph above ends with the verb **"suffice."** It might be tempting to write, "...where one well-chosen word would **be sufficient."**

That phrase adds only one word to the sentence, but consider that the addition of one extra word per sentence in a 10-page essay leads to a total of 120–150 extra words. That's nearly half a page!

If you remember that your essay is supposed to be painless (maybe even enjoyable) to read, you can begin to appreciate the harm wasting words can do—especially in situations, like college application essays or widescale writing assessments, in which you know that your essay will be one of hundreds of essays that are read. You want your essay to be fresh and new.

Exercise 2: Using the Concise Word

Below is a list of 20 phrases or expressions—some of them fairly common—that could be expressed more powerfully and more clearly in a single word. Write that single word.

Note some of the wordier expressions might sound more formal, and there might be times when such expressions will come in handy, but beware of overusing them or using them in inappropriate contexts and making your writing not formal, but stuffy.

Example: at the present time   *now*

1. make adjustments   _____
2. give instruction to   _____
3. make mention of   _____
4. in order to   _____
5. is reflective of   _____
6. can be compared to   _____
7. is capable of   _____
8. at this point   _____
9. ballpark figure   _____
10. by and large   _____
11. close proximity   _____
12. fresh-baked   _____
13. gathered together   _____
14. most complete   _____
15. past history   _____
16. the reason is because   _____
17. viable alternative   _____
18. adequate number of   _____
19. as a consequence of   _____
20. despite the fact that   _____

Exercise 3: Revising for Conciseness

The following letter does a fair job of establishing its purpose and communicating the necessary information, but it still uses too many vague and/or wordy constructions that need to be fixed. Revise the letter.

Roger Wibbat
197 Wonilotsamunni Road
Upper Spalding, MN

Office of Undergraduate Admissions
Possum Point University
P.O. Box 71356
Possum Point, AR

Dear Admissions Officer:

I am a fifteen-year-old tenth-grader who goes to Upper Scalding Regional High School here in Upper Scalding, Minnesota, and I am seriously considering a career in journalism. To pursue this goal, I would like to attend a college that offers a major either in journalism itself or in communications with a concentration in journalism. Both my current English teacher, Ms. Beardsley, and my guidance counselor, Mr. Reed, tell me that this is a wise course of action.

That is why I am writing to you today.

I know that Possum Point University in Possum Point, Arkansas, offers majors in both journalism and communications. A friend of mine who graduated last year and is now a freshman at Possum Point says you have a creative writing concentration in your communications program, and an MFA (Master of Fine Arts) in Creative Writing in your graduate school. This is good because, even though I want to be a journalist, I think I might also want to write at least one novel. Many journalists do. I believe Stephen Crane was a journalist as well as a fiction writer, and I am sure he is not the only one.

Before I can decide whether or not to attend Possum Point University—actually, before I decide whether or not I even want to apply to PPU—I think I need to look at your catalogue and see what the requirements for your degree programs are, what your tuition etc. expenses are, and what your entrance requirements are (like high school GPA—grade point average—SAT or ACT scores, etc.).

I also need information about financial aid (scholarships, loans, on-campus work study, etc.).

After I look at the catalogue, I know I will want to visit your campus. I could probably stay with my friend who is a freshman there and maybe even attend some classes with him.

I have wanted to be a writer all of my life, and I really think attending Possum Point University will be a big step in achieving that goal.

Thank-you for your time, and I look forward to hearing from you.

Sincerely,
Roger Wibbat

P.S.
Please send me a current undergraduate catalogue. You can send it to me at the above address.

Revision:

Fun With Idioms, Slang, and Clichés

An **idiom** is a popular expression, understood by most native speakers, that does not make literal sense. That means that if you examine the expression's grammar, sentence structure, word order, or the meaning of the individual words, the expression as a whole means something different than the individual words.

For example, the meanings of the expressions "it rings a bell" (sounds familiar), and to be "in the doghouse" (some kind of mild trouble) have no clear relationship to what the words and phrases mean literally. The problem with idioms is that your reader has to know the meaning of the expression before reading your piece. He or she has no resources, dictionary or encyclopedia, to explain an unfamiliar idiom, nor should he or she have to go to such great lengths to understand your writing to begin with. Remember that your writing is supposed to be painless to read. Idioms also lend a slightly informal or conversational tone to your writing. They are not really appropriate for formal, academic settings.

A **cliché** is any expression—idiomatic or not—that has been used so often that it has become almost a stock phrase. The problem with clichés is that they are too familiar. The writer has not really thought about what he or she is saying and has not attempted to find the best way to say it.

Slang expressions are similar to idioms with the exception that slang usually applies to an even narrower audience. Whereas many idioms can be understood by nearly every speaker of American English, slang changes with a person's region, age, level of education, income, race, religion, etc. Slang is also informal and inappropriate in any formal or academic setting.

Some readers might not understand your use of idioms or slang.

Exercise 4: Translating Idioms, Clichés, and Slang

The following list of twenty expressions contains idioms, clichés, and slang. In each case, consider what the expression means, and write a standard American English "translation" of the expression. If you cannot figure out what the expression means, leave the space blank, but consider how your use of similar expressions might interfere with your reader's ability to understand your writing.

1. All ears

2. An arm and a leg

3. At the end of your rope

4. Back on [one's] feet

5. Bend over backwards

6. Burn out

7. Cold feet

8. Couch potato

9. Cut and dried

10. Doctor [something] up

11. Dry run

12. Lemon

13. No-brainer

14. Nuke (two meanings)

15. Out of the woods

16. Play it by ear

17. Snail mail

18. Test the waters

19. The Man

20. Take the bull by the horns

Avoiding and Correcting Malapropisms

A **malapropism** is the misuse of a word or the use of an incorrect word for the context, mostly because the word used and the intended word are similar in spelling or pronunciation. For example, in a recent television commercial, one employee informs his co-worker that they receive *fringe* benefits, not *French* benefits. The use of "French" in this context is a malapropism.

Malapropisms commonly result from overusing the thesaurus to expand your vocabulary, and using synonyms with which you are not familiar. They can also be a symptom of careless listening.

Exercise 5: Correcting Malapropisms

Each of the twenty sentences below contains at least one malapropism. Define the word that is used incorrectly and write the correct word.

1. Nuclear physics is beyond most people's apprehension.

Definition:

Correction:

2. We need an energy bill that encourages consumption.

Definition:

Correction:

3. She'll think of something; she's the most remorseful person I know.

Definition:

Correction:

4. We are making steadfast progress.

Definition:

Correction:

5. We cannot let terrorists and rogue nations hold this nation hostile or hold our allies hostile.

Definition:

Correction:

6. I am mindful not only of preserving executive powers for myself, but for my predecessors as well.

Definition:

Correction:

7. The stories of Mark Twain are full of interesting caricatures.

Definition:

Correction:

8. Politicians understand the importance of bondage between a mother and child.

Definition:

Correction:

9. That new adventure novel is a real cliff-dweller.

Definition:

Correction:

10. Dad says the monster is just a pigment of my imagination.

Definition:

Correction:

11. Fine furniture at reasonable prices: antique, colonial, and temporary.

Definition:

Correction:

12. Look at that diamond pendulum around that man's neck.

Definition:

Correction:

13. He's a wolf in cheap clothing.

Definition:

Correction:

14. When we built our house, we paid to have extra installation put in the attic.

Definition:

Correction:

15. Michelangelo painted the Sixteenth Chapel.

Definition:

Correction:

16. Psychics claim to have extra-century perception.

Definition:

Correction:

17. In the Olympic Games, Greeks ran races, jumped, hurled the biscuits, and threw the java.

Definition:

Correction:

18. Julius Caesar extinguished himself on the battlefields of Gaul.

Definition:

Correction:

19. *Don't* is an example of a contraption.

Definition:

Correction:

20. We had a longer holiday than usual this year because the school was closed for altercations.

Definition:

Correction:

Writing Opportunity: *The Homework Essay: Explaining an Insight*

"Insight" is the word that describes your deeper understanding of something. In a sense, it is the ultimate goal of education: not for you to *know* facts and be able to recite them, but to *understand* principles and ideas and use your understanding to formulate new principles and ideas.

When you explain your insight on a topic, you provide your readers with a new and interesting way of looking at that topic.

This means that you might challenge a traditional view. You might explain the deeper understanding of something based on your own experience or study. You might focus on one aspect of a topic that hasn't really been examined before and show how it is misunderstood—or not really understood at all.

At its basic root, a research paper is an explanation of your insight accompanied by a detailed discussion of the reading, viewing, interviewing, etc., that helped you arrive at that insight. The important first step, then, is to think about something in a way that no one has explicitly taught you, but that you have developed on your own, and to explain that to your reader.

While the information you are communicating in this type of essay is of primary importance, voice and tone are also very important because they are the traits that allow you to convey your attitude toward your subject as well as your attitude toward your reader. In this assignment, you are asked to state and develop some insights of your own.

Step 1: *Choose and narrow your topic*
Think about a topic you know more about than most of your classmates, something about which you will be able to share new information or a new viewpoint.

After deciding on a topic, remember what you learned in Trait One of this book, that an important part of developing your topic is deciding what *one* aspect of the topic you are going to discuss. Remember that your goal is to leave your reader with *one* new thought, not a whole encyclopedia of insight.

Step 2: *Draft your thesis*
Write a single sentence that states your insight, or the new view or information you are going to share.

> Example:
>
> Most people, including many teachers and self-proclaimed "scholars," do not understand that William Shakespeare was not a literary luminary or cultural icon of his age, but an insignificant, popular playwright much more similar to the writers of today's television potboilers than Nobel-prize winning "literature."

Step 3: *Brainstorm and jot down your supporting details*
This is a step you should be familiar with by now. Think. Brainstorm. Take notes. What evidence do you have to support your claim? What examples of plots and characters from which plays will you offer as examples and evidence? How much background information will you have to share before you can begin to explain *your* insight?

> **Time Clue:** Assuming that you have been given one week for this assignment, you should devote two or three days to these first three steps.

Step 4: *Draft your outline*

Think like your intended reader. What is a logical order in which to present your evidence?

Time Clue: If you have done a thorough job in step 3, it should not take more than a day to plan and organize your essay.

Step 5: *Write your first draft*

Step 6: *Revise and rewrite*

Set your draft aside for the night. Then, read it critically and make all necessary revisions.

Before completing your final draft, show your draft to one or two other people and take their comments into consideration.

Step 7: *Your essay is finished. Submit it.*

Trait Six

Voice

TRAIT SIX:
VOICE

Establishing the
Writer-Reader Relationship

At the Novice Writer stage, you were told that the differences in meaning between the terms Tone and Voice were so subtle that these terms meant essentially the same thing. Now you will begin to learn what those subtle differences are so that, as you develop your skill as a writer, you will be able to manipulate both.

The effect created by your word choice and sentence structure is your voice. A good way to think about voice is to ask yourself, "What kind of person do I want to sound like?" (Or, after drafting your essay, read it aloud and ask yourself, "What kind of person do I sound like?") Do you sound (or want to sound) honest, condescending, anxious, authoritative, etc.? Voice, then, helps to establish the relationship between the writer and his or her audience.

Tone, on the other hand, refers to the writer's attitude toward his or her subject matter; for example, formal and informal. An essay may convey a sincere tone toward its topic, thus telling the reader that the material is to be taken seriously. Conversely, the writer may ridicule his or her subject matter while remaining respectful to his reader.

Again, the situation, or *exigence,* and the purpose for writing are also important considerations when determining what tone and voice to create.

Exigence is the official term for the situation or the circumstances that motivate you to write.

List at least five situations you have encountered which could have motivated you to write something: a letter of complaint or praise, an e-mail asking for more information, etc. It does not matter whether you actually wrote anything in response to the situation; simply use your experience to list the situation and what writing might have been appropriate.

Example:

When my package arrived, it did not contain everything I ordered. I could have written an e-mail inquiring about the rest of my order and complaining that there was no explanation included with the invoice.

1.

2.

3.

4.

5.

Tone and Voice are usually discussed in terms similar to the following:

informal, conversational	formal, respectful, academic
light, humorous, comic	serious
personal, subjective	impersonal, objective
casual, offhanded	fervent, passionate
plain, simple	ornate, elaborate

Remember that tone indicates your attitude toward your subject while voice establishes your attitude toward your subject.

For each of the situations you listed in the previous exercise, list who was (or would have been) the audience and what tone was (or would have been) most appropriate.

Example:

> **Audience:** *customer service*
> **Tone:** *personal, formal, serious*

1. **Audience:**
   Tone:

2. **Audience:**
   Tone:

3. **Audience:**
   Tone:

4. **Audience:**
   Tone:

5. **Audience:**
   Tone:

Make Yours Better!

Notice that the lack of a consistent voice actually makes it more difficult to follow the writer's argument or understand the main point. Look for places where the voice changes from essentially academic and neutral to almost offensive.

▨ This essay begins in a neutral, objective tone. The last two sentences suggest that the author will present evidence supporting both sides of this controversial issue.

As public schools in the United States become more crowded and need more money, many people are looking for new ways to educate their children. One solution that has been proposed involves the "education voucher." A voucher is a document allowing a student to attend a school other than the one to which he or she is assigned. Some people feel that vouchers take away from the public schools, while others say that vouchers let students and parents seek the best educational experience. Which is the best option?

A voucher works based on tax dollars. The tax dollars that normally a person living in that area pays, that go to schools in that area, are now given to the person so that his or her kids can attend a school of choice. When people have more choice about where to educate their children, schools have to work harder to attract the kids. No one can deny that this will make them better and stronger.

▨ As the essay goes on, the writer loses control of the neutral tone. Opinions begin to sneak in.

Also, schools are no longer racially divided based on neighborhoods that are made up of one race only, because the students going to the school are from all different neighborhoods. Only racist fools would fail to see the benefits in this.

▨ In the fourth paragraph, the writer sounds defensive. Rather than bringing up ideas and refuting them with facts, the writer provides the opinion of an organization without explaining why that organization has any authority or credibility.

Maybe you think this would isolate "minority" students, but minorities can get the most out of school vouchers. Groups like the Alliance for the Separation of School and State believe that because the government is not allowed to give students a moral education, it is not giving them a full education. The Alliance even says poor students are the worst-treated of all students when it comes to moral education.

▨ In the fifth paragraph, the author attempts a return to neutrality by bringing up the second side of the debate.

On the other hand, the National Education Association (NEA) says that school vouchers may harm disadvantaged students. This closed-minded group, made up mostly of teachers, claims that in states where vouchers are in place, there are different rules for public and private schools. The NEA also believes that public schools that are in trouble do not benefit from vouchers. While the Alliance for the Separation of School and State is supported by parents concerned about their children's education, the NEA is made up of teachers who want to keep their jobs, so of course, according to many critics, the NEA will be against anything that takes money away from them.

Just like in everything else, money is at the root of this problem. Money is the big issue for school vouchers, whether someone's tax dollars, a teacher's salary, or money for resources for a school. Should the government tell people how to spend money on education, or should the taxpayer who earned the money decide? Either way, the debate over school vouchers will likely not be ending any time soon.

Opinions are still clearly present, however.

■ During the argumentative previous paragraphs, the writer's language became more and more informal. Now the tone seems biased. In addition, the writer has not really analyzed the evidence presented. As a result, the conclusion is unsatisfying.

Essay Critique

It is difficult to say what the purpose of this essay is. From the introduction, we expect a balanced presentation of two sides of an issue. Instead, the writer tries to convince us that one side is more correct than the other. He or she needs to carefully monitor the language of the passage to be sure it is calm and neutral. Also, every statement should be backed up by a fact; ideas without support are opinions, and should be left out of the essay.

This essay receives a score of ④ on the:

Voice Rubric

8 = Self-conscious attempts at narrative voice result in either stilted or overblown usage. Problems in conventions, word choice, and sentence structure appear that are the result of attempts at voice.

7 = ADVANCING
A narrative voice appropriate to the topic, purpose, and audience is suggested, but inconsistently controlled—for the most part understated.

6 = The narrative voice of the essay is either inconsistent or not fully appropriate for the topic, purpose, and audience (e.g. an ironic, humorous tone for a serious subject, vitriol to a person in authority, etc.). Language is imprecise and inconsistently controlled.

5 = The essay shows strong evidence of an attempt to create a narrative voice, but the effect is not yet fully achieved, or reflects the writer's only voice—regardless of topic, purpose, or audience.

④ = DEVELOPING
A narrative voice is suggested, but inconsistently controlled, and may not be appropriate to the topic, purpose, and audience.

Examining Samples of a Variety of Tones and Voices

The language choices you make can create a wide range of voices and tones for any given piece of writing, and these different voices and tones are what will give your writing its individual impact.

Look, for example, at the variety of ways you can communicate to your teacher how you feel about receiving a disappointing grade on an important project. Notice how each expression reflects a different level of respect for the teacher and attitude toward the grade.

- I can't believe you gave me a D- on my project. You couldn't have looked at it very closely, and you obviously don't care how hard I worked on it.

- To give a D- to a project of this quality indicates that the scorer gave the work a mere casual glance instead of a close perusal, and certainly did not take into consideration the amount of time and effort that went into the project's completion.

- Anyone who would give this project a D- is just lazy and mean.

- I cannot help but wonder whether you found any strengths in my project at all, and whether any consideration of the amount of time and effort I put into it are reflected in this D-.

- I must admit that I am somewhat surprised by this grade. I spent a considerable amount of time and energy on this project, and thought it had some pretty good aspects.

- I'm shocked by this grade. I worked really hard, and I thought it was good.

- Could we have a conference to discuss exactly why I received the grade I did despite how hard I worked on this?

Each expression creates a different emotional and intellectual tone relative to the grade and the recipient's response thereto. In other words, the language style of each expression reflects a different attitude to the basic information.

Examining Those Factors That Help to Determine Voice

Examine each of the above examples to determine what is the writer's attitude toward the teacher and the grade. In the following samples, indicate the writer's attitude and how he or she conveys that attitude in the example.

Sample A:

I can't believe you gave me a D- on my project. You couldn't have looked at it very closely, and you obviously don't care how hard I worked on it.

What is the writer's attitude toward the grade?

What is the writer's attitude toward the teacher?

Which words help the writer convey these attitudes?

Sample B:

To give a D- to a project of this quality indicates that the scorer gave the work a mere casual glance instead of a close perusal, and certainly did not take into consideration the amount of time and effort that went into the project's completion.

What is the writer's attitude toward the grade?

What is the writer's attitude toward the teacher?

Which words help the writer convey these attitudes?

Sample C:

Anyone who would give this project a D– is just lazy and mean.

What is the writer's attitude toward the grade?

What is the writer's attitude toward the teacher?

Which words help the writer convey these attitudes?

Sample D:

I cannot help but wonder whether you found any strengths in my project at all, and whether any consideration of the amount of time and effort I put into it are reflected in this D-.

What is the writer's attitude toward the grade?

What is the writer's attitude toward the teacher?

Which words help the writer convey these attitudes?

Sample E:

I must admit that I am somewhat surprised by this grade. I spent a considerable amount of time and energy on this project, and thought it had some pretty good aspects.

What is the writer's attitude toward the grade?

What is the writer's attitude toward the teacher?

Which words help the writer convey these attitudes?

Sample F:

I'm shocked by this grade. I worked really hard, and I thought it was good.

What is the writer's attitude toward the grade?

What is the writer's attitude toward the teacher?

Which words help the writer convey these attitudes?

Sample G:

Could we have a conference to discuss exactly why I received the grade I did despite how hard I worked on this?

What is the writer's attitude toward the grade?

What is the writer's attitude toward the teacher?

Which words help the writer convey these attitudes?

Make certain your tone is appropriate for your audience.

Exercise 1: Experimenting with a Variety of Narrative Voices

Decide why the tone of each of the following brief passages might be inappropriate for its audience and purpose, and then rewrite it to make it more appropriate.

1. Passage 1

It doesn't take a rocket scientist to know you're supposed to read the fine print before you sign a contract.

Problem:

Revision:

2. Passage 2

I find it appropriate, in these days following the annual celebration of my birth, to express my gratitude to you for the token of your affection, which you bestowed upon me on that day.

Problem:

Revision:

3. Passage 3

There's lots of reasons I'd like a job at your company. First of all, the pay is great—not to mention all the perks and benes.

Problem:

Revision:

Exercise 2: Choosing a Tone Appropriate for the Audience

Using the following information, compose several one- or two-paragraph passages answering the question, "WHY DO YOU WANT TO ATTEND WESTPHALIA COLLEGE?" Be certain to make each version of your passage appropriate to the given situation.

Information:

Name of school: Westphalia College

Setting/location: Urban/downtown San Chianti

Size: Small

Student Body: 1,000; 3:1 male-to-female ratio

Available Majors: English literature, ancient history, music appreciation.
Co-curricular Activities: Chess team (north-east regional champions), water aerobics, monthly newsletter, CB (Citizens Band) Radio club

Distinguished Alumni: Patricia Cunegonde, voted "Best Actress" three consecutive years by the Brazilian Independent Film Association; Dr. Martin Pangloss, developer of nasal decongestant spray for elephants; Marion Dalley, former mayor of San Chianti, acquitted of thirteen counts of fraud, embezzlement, and misuse of governmental authority, and author of the bestselling *I Got Away With It; You Can Too.*

Distinguished Faculty: None

Campus Life Highlights: Annual midnight barefoot marathon, annual frozen fish toss, free monthly movies, seasonal chess pep rallies.

Fun Facts: Voted 372nd Most Beautiful Campus in the Mid West. Boasts highest percentage of students with O- blood in thirteen states. President William Henry Harrison scheduled to speak at first annual commencement (June 1841) but died two months earlier.

1. Situation 1

This essay is part of your application packet to Westphalia College, which is your first-choice school.

Version 1:

2. Situation 2

You are responding to a fellow student who considers Westphalia to be an inferior college.

Version 2:

3. Situation 3

You are writing to a family friend who is hurt that you do not want to attend the college at which she is a professor.

Version 3:

4. Situation 4

You are writing to your parents who have told you that Westphalia is too expensive, and you must go to a local college.

Version 4:

5. Situation 5

You have no desire to attend Westphalia, but are writing to win a satire contest your high school is holding.

Version 5:

Writing Opportunity: *Profiling a Person or a Place*

A profile is a focused description of a person or a place. You might, for example, focus on someone's interesting career, hobby, or lifestyle. You might write about someone who has made a major contribution to his or her community, someone who has faced a tremendous challenge, or someone who played an important role in your growing up.

To profile a place, you might want to consider taking readers someplace exotic and exciting—where you yourself faced adventure or learned an important lesson. You might encourage readers to visit a favorite place (or discourage them from visiting someplace you found disappointing). Just remember that your focus is on the place you are profiling and the aspect(s) of the place you are focusing on, not on your personal view or evaluation.

You may need to do some research—a magazine article or two, a simple web search for necessary factual information—but the basis of your profile should be your own personal knowledge of, and experiences with, the person or place you are profiling.

While all of the traits of powerful essays are important here, tone and voice are especially important because they will allow you to subtly indicate your attitude toward the person or place you are profiling without inserting first person observations. For example, instead of writing, "I admire so-and-so..." you will write, "So-and-so possesses countless admirable qualities..."

Step 1: *Decide on the person or place you want to profile
and why*

Take the first day of your assignment period and look through photo
albums, diaries, or journals you may have kept, and jot down the
names of all of the people and all of the places you might want to
profile. Also, jot down your reasons for considering each of these
people and places, and some essential details you would most likely
include in your profile.

Then choose the person or place about whom you know you have
the most to say, or the one that most interests and fascinates you.

> **Hint:** Even though you will ultimately write about only
> one person or place, at this stage, it is really in your best
> interest to brainstorm and develop as many possibilities as
> you can. You do not want to invest too much time on your
> "only idea" only to find out that you simply don't have much
> to say. It is much better to be able to choose from among
> several possibilities.

Step 2: *Draft your thesis statement*

In a single sentence, state the person or place you are profiling and
the focus of the profile.

> Example:
>
> Chesterfield Pinkus, R.N., the first male school nurse in the
> Highland Consolidated School District, is an unsung hero
> in the ongoing fight against gender discrimination in the
> workplace.

Notice how the writer has identified Chesterfield Pinkus as the
person he or she is going to profile, and the focus of the profile—
Pinkus' role in the battle against gender discrimination in the
workplace. In addition, the idea that Pinkus represents a unique
twist on the gender-equity issue—a man struggling for a place in a
predominantly female profession—is strongly suggested.

Step 3: *Brainstorm (again) and jot down more supporting details*

You have already brainstormed some before you chose your subject. Take some time now, however, to make certain that you have notes on every relevant aspect of your subject—the answers to the five Ws and one H.

Here is where you might need to do some research to find any precise dates, full and correct names of schools, names and titles of other people pertinent to your topic, etc.

Time Clue: For a one-week essay, give yourself two or three days for this information-gathering stage. As you have already seen, if you do a thorough job in these early steps, the actual writing of the essay is a relatively easy and painless task.

Step 4: *Organize*

Think like your intended reader. What is a logical order in which to discuss your ideas? In our example, would we need to go into a full biography of Pinkus? Would it be more effective to start somewhere in the middle of Pinkus' life and career and then use flashbacks to provide the necessary background information, or would it be clearer for our reader to go in chronological order?

In an essay like this, your decisions about organization must strike a balance between your need for clarity and your desire for drama.

Time Clue: Allow yourself one day to draft as many versions of an outline as you need.

Step 5: *Write your first draft(s)*

Because this profile allows for a variety of different approaches, write as many first drafts as you have outlines. This is not too time-consuming a step if you have been careful to gather sufficient information, and have already thought carefully about how to present the information.

Time Clue: Again, writing the first draft—even two or three versions—should not take more than one day.

Step 6: *Revise and rewrite*

Set your drafts aside for the night. You can use that time to ask one or two other people to read them over and critique them.

Then read them as if you were the person to whom you are writing and decide which is the clearest, most complete, and most interesting for your reader. Rewrite that draft, fixing any of the problems you found when you read it (or were pointed out to you).

Step 7: Your profile is done. Submit it.

Appendix One:

Scoring Guide for the Developing Level

DEVELOPMENT AND ELABORATION

8 = The main idea of the essay is clear. There is almost enough information for a full and complete discussion, but the reader is left with a few unanswered questions. Minor irrelevancies, redundancies, and superfluencies weaken the overall impact of the essay.

7 = **ADVANCING**
The main idea of the essay is clear. Every supporting point is supported and details are elaborated upon, but minor irrelevancies, redundancies, and superfluencies weaken the overall impact of the essay.

6 = The main idea of the essay is clear, most supporting points are elaborated upon, but some of the information presented is notably irrelevant, redundant, and superfluous.

5 = The main idea of the essay is clear, but the overall discussion is weakened by inconsistent development and elaboration. Some Supporting points tend to be underdeveloped (too few details, examples, anecdotes, supporting facts, etc.). Some minor irrelevancies likewise weaken the essay.

4 = **DEVELOPING**
The main idea of the essay is suggested. There are supporting details with some elaboration, but supporting points are underdeveloped. Some of the points or development my be tangential or irrelevant to the topic, purpose, and audience.

ORGANIZATION

8 = There is a strong attempt at an original organizational plan. Minor jumps or gaps are the result of experimenting with a more sophisticated plan.

7 = **ADVANCING**

The organizational plan shows strong evidence of moving beyond mere formula (e.g. the five-paragraph essay). Jumps or gaps are the result of experimenting with a more sophisticated plan.

6 = The organizational plan of the essay is clear and consistently applied and shows evidence of moving beyond mere formula (e.g. the five-paragraph essay).

5 = The organizational plan of the essay is clear and consistently applied but is obvious and/or formulaic (e.g., the five-paragraph essay), thus limiting the essay's overall effectiveness.

4 = **DEVELOPING**

An appropriate but obvious organizational plan is apparent and generally followed, but jumps or gaps distract the reader.

SENTENCE STRUCTURE AND VARIETY

8 = There is evidence of an awareness of audience, purpose, tone, and the demands of the topic in sentence structure choices. Minor lapses in tone and style—on the sentence level—weaken the overall effect.

7 = **ADVANCING**
The writer has made intentional sentence formation choices for the sake of clarity and impact, but the resulting tone and voice are not fully appropriate to the audience, purpose, and topic. Minor problems in structure, grammar, and/or word choice make the essay less effective than it might be.

6 = The writer has made a concerted effort to use a variety of structures to enhance the effectiveness of the essay. Sentences are clear, but minor problems resulting from an attempt to use more sophisticated structures detract from the overall effectiveness of the essay.

5 = There is an attempt to vary sentence length and structure, but it appears to be variety for variety's sake rather than topic, purpose, audience, and voice determining appropriate sentence structure. Minor problems in structure, grammar, and/or word choice make them less effective than they might be. These errors can be corrected with minor revision (insertion of words, creation of appositives and/or subordinate clauses, etc.).

4 = **DEVELOPING**
There is evidence of experimentation with sentence variety, but this variety is forced and may result in awkward and inappropriate constructions.

CONVENTIONS OF WRITTEN ENGLISH

8 = Infrequent, minor surface errors suggest the need for careful editing, but do not require any revision in order to correct.

7 = **ADVANCING**
Infrequent surface errors suggest the need for careful editing and some revision of the essay.

6 = Infrequent minor surface errors suggest an attempt to experiment with more sophisticated language. These may distract the reader and require substantial revision of the essay.

5 = Essay is largely free of basic surface errors. Errors that do appear (semi-colon, complex subject-verb agreement, etc.) suggest an attempt to experiment with more sophisticated language and may interfere with the reader's understanding, requiring extensive revision.

4 = **DEVELOPING**
Essay is largely free of basic surface errors (spelling, elementary punctuation, capitalization, etc.), but correctness of language is largely governed by simplicity of language.

WORD CHOICE

8 = For the most part, the writer has chosen vivid, powerful nouns and verbs, but still relies somewhat on obviously unfamiliar words from vocabulary lists and thesauri. Figurative devices (similes, metaphors, allusions) are original, but inappropriate to the other aspects of the essay (subject, occasion, audience, purpose).

7 = **ADVANCING**
Attempts at vividness might result in strained or forced usage – "thesaurus-itis". Use of figurative language (similes, metaphors, allusions) is experimental and therefore might be unoriginal, out-of-place, or forced.

6 = Word choice is at times vivid and strong, but occasionally lapses into the weak and general. The essay may exhibit signs of "thesaurus-itis:" words appear straight from the pages of Roget, but do not quite fit, are not used quite appropriately. The use of figurative language (similes, metaphors, allusions) is experimental and therefore might be unoriginal, out-of-place, or forced.

5 = Word choice shows strong attempts at vividness, but vague and inexact language predominates. Figurative language (similes, metaphors, allusions) is unoriginal, and does not really contribute to the overall effect of the essay.

4 = **DEVELOPING**
Attempts at vividness are more frequent and intentional, but miss the mark, often resulting in clichés, awkward constructions, and an overuse of adjective-noun and adverb-verb phrases, especially overuse of amplifiers like "very," "truly," etc.

VOICE

8 = Self-conscious attempts at narrative voice result in either stilted or overblown usage. Problems in conventions, word choice, and sentence structure appear that are the result of attempts at voice.

7 = **ADVANCING**

A narrative voice appropriate to the topic, purpose, and audience is suggested, but inconsistently controlled—for the most part understated.

6 = The narrative voice of the essay is either inconsistent or not fully appropriate for the topic, purpose, and audience (e.g. an ironic, humorous tone for a serious subject, vitriol to a person in authority, etc.). Language is imprecise and inconsistently controlled.

5 = The essay shows strong evidence of an attempt to create a narrative voice, but the effect is not yet fully achieved, or reflects the writer's only voice—regardless of topic, purpose, or audience.

4 = **DEVELOPING**

A narrative voice is suggested, but inconsistently controlled, and may not be appropriate to the topic, purpose, and audience.

Appendix Two:

Introduction to Logical Fallacies

Just as successfully arguing or discussing a point depends on your ability to use language appropriately, it is also important for you to be able to argue appropriately. You will find yourself writing much stronger papers (and receiving higher grades) if you learn to avoid some of the most common pitfalls:

1. Factual Error

Just as the name suggests, this is simply having incorrect information in support of any of your points of argument. It almost goes without saying that you cannot hope to establish the validity of your thesis if you support it with misinformation. The only solution for factual error is to do careful research from reliable sources, to read and listen carefully, to take careful notes, and to verify your most pertinent information with two or more sources.

2. Appeal to Unreliable Authority

This fallacy is closely related to the factual error. An unreliable authority is anyone who is not really in a position to make the claims or offer the advice he or she is making. It is the reason every research handbook you ever read will stress that you be careful about the quality of the sources you use.

There are several ways to assess the reliability of a source. Print sources are obviously the easiest. Scholarly or academic journals, and trade or professional journals are obviously reliable sources of information. Respected news magazines and newspapers are clearly more reliable than sensational tabloids. Books published by legitimate publishers are "safer" than self-published or "e-books." If you need to, search for the author on the Internet and see what else he or she has written, what his or her professional credentials are, what has been written about him or her, etc.

If you are doing Internet research, make certain that you can find the name of the person who wrote the information. "Anonymous" information is always suspect. Use only recognized, respected, and authoritative sites.

Finally, never rely on a single source for your most important information. If you cannot find at least one more source to verify a "fact," then consider it suspect and build your argument without it.

3. Flawed Inductive Argument

In Trait Two, you learned that inductive reasoning is the process of finding patterns in known cases and then using those patterns to infer new information about unknown cases. For example, while studying your vocabulary, you begin to notice that all of the words you encounter that end in *ize* are verbs. Moreover, you notice that the roots of these words are all adjectives to which the *ize* has been added. You conclude, therefore, that adding *ize* to the end of an adjective turns that adjective into a verb.

A flawed inductive argument is, quite simply, an invalid conclusion, either because it is based on errors in fact (e.g.: NOT all *ize* words are adjectives turned into verbs) or are the result of jumping to a hasty conclusion based on too few examples.

The remedy is to continue brainstorming examples or to continue your research until you have gathered enough accurate information to demonstrate the validity of your thesis.

4. Flawed Deduction

In Trait Two, you also learned that deductive reasoning uses an established general principle (e.g.: dew occurs when there is more moisture in the air than the air's temperature will allow it to hold) and one or more facts (e.g. it has been very humid all day, and now the temperature is falling) to make predictions (e.g. there will be dew on the ground this evening).

A flawed deductive argument is, again, an invalid conclusion, arrived at by using either an unsound general principle or committing one or more errors in fact.

For example (unsound general principle):

- Since attractive people are good, and unattractive people are evil, the beautiful Gretchen must be a good person, while her funny-looking brother, Hanson, must be a trouble maker.

- It may be true that Gretchen is pretty and Hanson funny-looking, but the basic principle that beauty equates to goodness and ugliness to evil is "true" only in fairy tales.

For example (errors in fact):

- I enjoy reading and watching plays written by Arthur Miller, so I will most likely enjoy *The Glass Menagerie*.

- The fact that this person likes Arthur Miller's plays will have no bearing on whether he or she will enjoy *The Glass Menagerie*, which was written by Tennessee Williams.

5. Burden of Proof

In preparation for the Writing Opportunity in Trait Four, we discussed the concept of "burden of proof," the idea that it is the person making the claim, or stating the thesis, who must demonstrate the validity of that thesis. In Trait Four, we talked in terms of a court trial in which the prosecution has the burden of proof. The prosecution is claiming that the defendant is guilty, so it is the prosecution's responsibility to prove it.

The fallacy associated with burden of proof is essentially assigning it to the wrong side of the argument, like the prosecution's claiming that since the defense did not prove the defendant's innocence, he must be guilty.

For example:

- In the evolution vs. creationism debate, *both sides* occasionally claim "victory" because no one has yet proven the "other side" to be true.

- Using the fact that no one has invented a time machine yet to "prove" that time travel is impossible.

The best ways to avoid a burden of proof fallacy are to be very careful to word your thesis in such a way that it can be positively proven and to make certain you offer examples and facts in support of your thesis. Do not simply assume the absence of argument is sufficient.

6. Jumping to a Hasty Generalization

Just as the expression "jumping to conclusions" suggests, this is simply the forming of a conclusion based on too little evidence, too few examples, or examples that are weak instead of compelling. The solution is, of course, to make sure you have a valid conclusion and then, find and present the best, most-compelling evidence, and to present as much as you can (short of driving your reader to distraction and filling pages and pages of repetitive information).

7. Error of Composition

Error of Composition is a little similar to Jumping to Conclusions. In Jumping to Conclusions, you arrive at a conclusion based on observation of too few examples. In Error of Composition, you take your understanding of the characteristics of a member of a group and arrive at a faulty conclusion about that group.

For example:

- The fact that the members of a chorus are all world-class, award-winning singers does not guarantee that they will be able to blend their voices into a world-class, award-winning chorus.

- The facts that, individually, sodium and chlorine are dangerous to humans does not mean that a combination of sodium and chlorine must be dangerous for humans. The combination of sodium and chlorine (sodium chloride) is simple table salt.

- The fact that a gasoline-powered lawn mower pollutes more than a gasoline-powered automobile does not necessarily mean that, collectively, lawn mowers cause more pollution than cars.

To avoid Errors of Composition in your essays and papers, first, ask yourself whether your conclusion *always and necessarily flows* from the specific facts. In most Errors of Composition, it won't. Secondly, do the research necessary to verify or refute your claim: statistically, how much total air pollution is caused by lawn mowers and, statistically, how much total air pollution is caused by cars, etc.

8. *Post hoc, ergo propter hoc*:

The Latin phrase is usually translated as "After this, therefore because of this." It is the erroneous assumption that simply because one thing happed *before* something else, it *caused* the something else.

For example:

- In the nineteenth and early twentieth centuries, doctors noticed that people who sat out in the night air, or left their windows open at night, often came down with malaria (which literally means "bad air"). They concluded that, since exposure to night air occurred before the malaria developed, it must have caused the malaria.

- In the Middle Ages, if a stranger arrived in a town and anything unusual happened in that town, it was naturally assumed that the arrival of the stranger caused the unusual occurrences.

- A person is caught outside in a winter rainstorm. The next morning he wakes up with a bad cold. He might conclude that getting wet the day before caused his cold, although medical science would disagree.

The safest way to avoid this fallacy in your writing is to continue your research to verify any cause and effect relationship you want to discuss.

9. Begging the Question

As you've probably noticed, all valid argument relies on a clear thesis statement and valid facts or examples in support of that thesis statement. We both agree that "A" is true. I can prove to you that "B" is true, and therefore you must admit the validity of "C."

However, what happens when I *assume* "A" to be true, you do not, and I offer no evidence, is called "Begging the Question."

For example:

- Since flowering trees are prettier than non-flowering trees, surely you'll agree that we must plant only flowering trees in our front yard. (The speaker here is *assuming* the person addressed agrees that flowering trees are prettier. He or she is begging the question).

The fallacy takes on real importance in arguments on political and/or moral issues. When one of the sides bases its argument on an *axiom*, a self-evident truth that does not "need" to be "proven," then real debate grinds to a halt.

For example:

- Since it is never right to kill a human being, the death penalty must be abolished. (That it is "never right to kill a human being" is a moral axiom. Many would disagree and say that wartime, self-defense, and euthanasia are examples of the justifiable killing of a human being.)

- Given Western Civilization's inherent superiority, it is vital that we help to civilize the rest of the world. (Again, many do not see "Western Civilization's inherent superiority," yet the speaker continues to the conclusion, assuming the axiom to be unchallenged and true.)

The only way to avoid Begging the Question in your writing is to make certain that your "truths" are indeed truths, that they have been established, and that you can support evidence for them. In a formal, academic essay or paper, it is never appropriate to base an argument on an axiom—a statement you assume to be true and that you assume your reader also takes as true.

10. Slippery Slope

The Slippery Slope is a fallacy in which a person asserts that some (usually horrible) consequence will inevitably result from some (usually minor) event without offering any evidence that the consequence is indeed inevitable. In most cases, the consequence is indeed possible, but there is a series of steps between the initial event and the horrible consequence.

For example:

- If we allow this land to be rezoned for commercial development, it won't be long until the entire highway is lined with smog-belching factories.

- First, we let a student representative on the curriculum review committee, and the next thing you know, we'll all be teaching from comic books.

To avoid the Slippery Slope in your writing, really examine the consequence you are predicting and consider how inevitable it really is. Also consider how many other things must happen before the consequence. If it's worth discussing at all, it's worth discussing the entire sequence of events.

Appendix Three:

Introduction to MLA Documentation

As you begin to use more outside sources for information and insight, it will become extremely important for you to learn how to handle those sources, to avoid charges of plagiarism and academic infringement. Please understand that such charges can have devastating consequences in college, graduate school, and professional life. Students have been placed on "academic probation," have been expelled from school, and have lost membership in student and professional societies as a result of charges of plagiarism. Professional writers have been fined and have actually lost their jobs as the result of charges of plagiarism. At the very least, college, graduate students, and professionals have accumulated tremendous legal bills defending themselves against these charges.

Your best defense, therefore, is to know how to present information from outside sources, how to quote appropriately, and how to document the information and sources you use.

Another benefit is that proper documentation of sources helps you to avoid the "Unreliable Authority" fallacy discussed in Appendix 2.

1. What is documentation?

Documentation is, quite simply, giving credit where credit is due. Imagine this: you tell a very funny joke to a friend. A little while later, you walk into a room and hear your friend tell *your* joke as if it were *his*. He gets the credit for making his audience laugh. At the very least, you would have expected your friend to say: "I heard the funniest joke from [insert your name here]" before telling the joke.

And that's essentially what documentation is: giving credit to the sources from which you got information for your paper or essay.

2. Why must I be so careful about documenting my sources?

To present someone else's words as if they were your words, or to present information you got from someone else without giving that person credit is

- unfair (We all want to be acknowledged for our work and our contribution to a project.)

- unethical (Professionals especially rely on receiving credit for their work because it is on the basis of that credit that they receive promotions, pay raises, and other opportunities to advance professionally. Non-professionals also rely on receiving credit for their work to qualify them for advanced study or to open professional opportunities for them.)

- illegal (The written ideas of others; their song lyrics; musical notations; painted, sculpted, photographed, or filmed artwork; their poetry, short stories, novels, plays, informative articles; etc., are all included in the definition of "intellectual property." Intellectual property is just as real as physical property, and it is protected by law. That's what a copyright is: the declaration that the holder of the copyright "owns" the right to make copies of the work, or to give permission to someone else to make copies. To violate a copyright is to steal someone else's property and is punishable by law: expulsion from school, lawsuit, fine, etc.).

Many people in the academic world consider plagiarism—the use of someone else's ideas or words without permission and without proper documentation—to be the worst crime that can be committed in academia.

3. What are the absolute basics of proper documentation?
At the very least, you must provide two types of documentation: the works cited page (or bibliography) and the in-text citation.

The Works Cited Page is a page at the end of your paper that lists every source of information you used in creating the essay, paper, report, or whatever. The format of this page will be determined by your instructor, your school, or the field of study in which you have done your research. In your English classes, foreign language classes, and most other humanities classes, you will use the format prescribed by the Modern Language Association (MLA).

The in-text citation is a note in the actual body of your paper that states where you got a particular bit of information or whose words you are quoting. Again, the format of this citation will be given to you.

4. Under what circumstances must I include a Works Cited Page in my essay or paper?
Every time you consult a source that is outside of your own body of knowledge, you should include a Works Cited Page at the end of your paper.

If you have consulted only one or two outside sources, and you refer specifically to these sources in the body of your paper, you might be able to justify eliminating the Works Cited Page, but it is best to err on the side of safety and include one.
Note: The title of the page is *Works Cited,* which implies that you include only those works for which you have an in-text citation. The issue then becomes: if you *consulted* a source and got information or ideas from it; and if you *presented* information from that source in your paper, you need to cite that source—and that source then needs to appear on your Works Cited Page.

5. What information must I include in the Works Cited Page?
Generally, the Works Cited Page provides your reader with the author, title, publication data, and copyright date of the sources from which you took information in the creation of your own work.

A works cited entry for a book would look like this:

> Last, First. Title of Book. City: Publishing Company, copyright.

> Pearl, Matthew. The Poe Shadow. New York: Random House, 2006.

A works cited entry for a magazine or newspaper article would look like this:

> Last, First. "Title of Article" Name of Newspaper or Magazine date of issue (European style): page number.

> Conchina, Laura M. "Matthew Pearl's Sophomore Novel Triumphs" Literary Weekly Review 22 June 2006: 32.

> Dunnel, Barbara. "Another Pearl of Great Price." New York Herald Journal 23 May 2006, natl.ed.: C8.

A works cited entry for a web site would look like this:

> Title of Article or Web Cite. Author or producer of web information, copyright. Universal Resource Locator (URL).

> Author Spotlight: Matthew Pearl. Random House, Inc., 2006. <http://www.randomhouse.com/author/results.pperl?authorid=23463>

Note 1: Every detail of the above format is important to replicate in your documentation. Where the prescribed format has a period, you must place a period. Where the format has a comma, you must place a comma, etc.

Note 2: While many printers and designers advise that underlining is stylistically bad (in print, underlining is a code for *italics*), the *MLA Handbook* recommends underlining material that is italicized in print.

Note 3: Because there are so many variations on the above types of sources, especially web sites and electronic sources, it is virtually impossible to "learn" every form. In addition, the forms are revised frequently. Rather than spend your time trying to memorize the format for each type of entry, find a good style sheet or handbook that provides examples of each type of source and learn how to follow it.

6. **Under what circumstances must I include an in-text citation in my essay or paper?**
The absolute and inviolable rule for citation is that you *must* cite the source for every bit of information you present that you received from someone else. This includes:

Direct quotations: Whenever you use the *exact* words of your source (even a phrase or a single word), you *must* put those words in quotation marks " ", and you *must* cite the source of the quotation. Here is where a statement of attribution is most warranted as well.

Make certain your own notes make it clear what information is paraphrased and where you have used the source's words.

Close paraphrases:
Even if you take the source's information and reformulate it in your own words, you *must* cite the fact that you got this particular bit of information from this particular source.

Summaries:
Just as with a paraphrase, even if you summarize a paragraph, chapter, or entire article or book, you must cite the source of the information.

7. Why must I use in-text citations for these uses?
The answer to this question involves exposing you to some hard truths about the academic world.

a. It's all about authority and credibility
The whole purpose of a research project is for you to learn something independently and then to demonstrate to someone else what you have learned. It makes sense that you will not learn much from someone who knows nothing about your topic. Likewise, you will not learn much from someone who is a chronic liar or who has some propagandistic agenda to meet. Therefore, any bit of information you get from an outside source must be subject to scrutiny. Are your sources reliable? Credible? Are the people you cite in a position to know what they are talking about? Are they likely to be honest and objective?

b. You are not (yet) an expert in your own right
This is not to say you know nothing, and it certainly does not take away your right to an opinion (see point **c** below), but compared to someone who has spent his or her life working and studying in the field you are researching, you are not an expert. That means that *your* reader is under no obligation to take what you say as valid simply because you have said it. Citing your sources tells your reader that you know what you are talking about because you consulted sources who know what they are talking about (see point **a** above).

c. You have the right to your opinion, but it needs to be an *informed* opinion
Most likely, you have already been in the position of having a discussion with someone who clearly did not know what he or she was talking about. It is frustrating. Here, this person is saying that such-and-such is so much better (or worse) than so-and-so, and you know that this person has no knowledge of, or experience with, either. Yet, this person will defend his or her position with the inevitable, "I have a right to my opinion."

And this is true. *But* that person's right to an "opinion" does not obligate you or anyone else to listen when it is clear that he or she has no basis for the "opinion." Therefore, if you want any of your own discussion to carry weight with your reader, if you want your own ideas to take on validity, if you want to start to become an expert in the subject you are researching, you begin by showing your reader that you are familiar with those who already are respected experts.

If you do not cite your sources, your paper is no better than one written by a student who did no research at all.

8. Doesn't that mean that *everything* in my paper will be cited and documented?
It does not. Remember in Trait One you worked on taking three types of notes in three different colors: information directly from your sources, your reaction to your sources, your own original thoughts. Only the first level—information from your sources—will be cited and documented. Since the "source" for your reactions and your original ideas is you, you have no source to document.

If, as you write the first draft of your paper, you find yourself citing and documenting every sentence, every paragraph, every bit of information and insight you present, you know that you have not contributed enough to the discussion. What you are writing, then, is an elementary-level report, not a thesis-based research paper.

9. So what information must I include in the in-text citation?
Compared to the variables and complexities of the Works Cited Page, the in-text citation is easy. Essentially, all you need is to place the author's last name and the page number from the source you are documenting after the quotation, paraphrase, or summary.

a. In-text citations from the sources you have listed on the Works Cited Page above would look like this:

(Pearl 87)

(Conchina 34)

(Dunnel C12)

If there is no stated author, then an abbreviated form of the title will be sufficient.

(Author Spotlight: Matthew Pearl)

These are the forms for citing *all* information from your sources, whether it be in the form of a direct quotation, paraphrase, or summary.

Important Variation: If you attribute a quotation or paraphrase to the source in the body of your paper, then you omit the author's name from the material in the parentheses.

For example:
(No attribution in the text):
Some scientists still cling to the theory that the moon is made of green cheese: "Clearly the quality of light the full moon casts on the landscape is consistent with sunlight reflecting off a huge cheese ball" (Stilton 293).

(Attribution in the text—direct quotation):
Some scientists still cling to the theory that the moon is made of green cheese. As Brie Stilton notes, "Clearly the quality of light the full moon casts on the landscape is consistent with sunlight reflecting off a huge cheese ball" (293).

(Attribution in the text—paraphrase):
Some scientists still cling to the theory that the moon is made of green cheese. Brie Stilton suggests that the light of the full moon is the type that would be created by sunlight reflecting off a ball of cheese (293).

When you have attributed the quotation to the source in the body of your paragraph, you do not need to repeat the author's name in the parenthetic citation.

Notice how the word "that" introduces a paraphrase, *not* a direct quotation.

Correct: Jane said, "I want to go home."
Correct: Jane said that she wanted to go home.
Incorrect: Jane said that, "I want to go home."

b. If you have more than one source by the same author on your Works Cited Page, follow the same logic about attribution and author's name and add an abbreviated version of the title of the specific source you are citing.

For example:
(No attribution in the text):
Some scientists still cling to the theory that the moon is made of green cheese: "Clearly the quality of light the full moon casts on the landscape is consistent with sunlight reflecting off a huge cheese ball" (Stilton, When it Sits on a Ritz 293).

(Attribution in the text—direct quotation):
Some scientists still cling to the theory that the moon is made of green

cheese. As Brie Stilton notes, "Clearly the quality of light the full moon casts on the landscape is consistent with sunlight reflecting off a huge cheese ball" (When it Sits on a Ritz 293).

(Attribution in the text—paraphrase):
Some scientists still cling to the theory that the moon is made of green cheese. Brie Stilton suggests that the light of the full moon is the type that could be created by sunlight reflecting off a ball of cheese (When it Sits on a Ritz 293).

Important Variation: If you choose to mention the title of the source in the body of the paragraph, then you do not need to repeat that information in the parentheses.

For example: Some scientists still cling to the theory that the moon is made of green cheese. In her memoir, When it Sits on a Ritz, astrolonomer-psychic Brie Stilton suggests that the light of the full moon is the type that could be created by sunlight reflecting off a ball of cheese (293).

Note the logic. Attribution, citation, and documentation formats are based on the principles of giving your reader all of the information he or she might need to locate the source and verify the accuracy of the information, while at the same time saving you from having to repeat author, title, and other publication data.

Note 1: As with the Works Cited Page formats, because there is so much variation in the types of sources, rather than trying to learn them all, it would be much better for you to get a good style sheet or handbook and learn how to follow the models.

Note 2: Again, note that there is no punctuation between the author's name and the page number, nor is the page number indicated by any abbreviation (pg., p., pp., etc.).